GURU

GURU

METAPHORS FROM A PSYCHOTHERAPIST

Sheldon B. Kopp

SCIENCE AND BEHAVIOR BOOKS

Palo Alto, California

The author gratefully acknowledges the permission granted by publishers and copyright holders to quote from the following works:

Winnie-the-Pooh by A. A. Milne; copyright 1926 by E. P. Dutton & Co.; renewal copyright 1954 by A. A. Milne. *Tales of the Hasidim: The Later Masters* by Martin Buber; copyright 1948 by Schocken Books, Inc. *The Prince* by Niccolo Machiavelli, trans. by Luigi Ricci, rev. by E. R. P. Vincent; publ. by Oxford University Press. *Basic Writings* by Chuang Tzu, trans. by Burton Watson; copyright 1964 by Columbia University Press. *Moral Essays* by Lucius Annaeus Seneca, trans. by John W. Basore; copyright 1928 by the Loeb Classical Library and Harvard University Press. From the *R. M. Bucke Society Newsletter-Review*, "The Spiritual Father in the Desert Tradition," 3:1. *The Desert Fathers*, ed. and trans. by Helen Waddell; copyright 1957 by the University of Michigan Press. "God Bless' the Child" by Arthur Herzog, Jr., and Billie Holiday; copyright by the Edward B. Marks Music Corporation. *The Morning Watch* by James Agee; copyright 1951 by Houghton Mifflin Co. *The Wisdom of Confucius* ed. by Lin Yutang; copyright 1938 by Random House. *The Collected Poems of Dylan Thomas*; copyright 1939, 1943, 1946 by New Directions Publishing Corp.; copyright 1952 by Dylan Thomas. *Three Ways of Thought in Ancient China* by Arthur Waley; copyright 1940 by Macmillan Co. *The Wizard of Oz* by L. Frank Baum; copyright 1956 by Reilly & Lee Co. *Selected Essays* by Michel de Montaigne, trans. by Charles Cotton and W. Hazlitt; copyright 1949 by Random House. *Meister Eckhart: A Modern Translation*, trans. By Raymond Bernard Blakney; copyright 1941 by Harper & Row.

The author would also like to thank the following publishers for allowing him to reprint or adapt material from the following works:

Psychology Today, "The Zaddik," May, 1969; "The Wizard of Oz Behind the Couch," March, 1970. *Voices*, "A Brief Essay on Not Getting to Know One Another," Fall, 1965; "The Wonderful Wizard," Spring, 1968; "The Refusal to Mourn," Spring, 1969; "Hasidic Teaching: Being with the Other," Summer, 1969; "Hard Travelin', Lord," Winter, 1970; *Psychological Perspectives*, "A Time for Priests, A Time for Shamans," Spring, 1970.

Library of Congress Card Number 71-142730

ISBN 0-8314-0025-0

To Marjorie

She loves me without trying to change me.
In this way, she helps me to become who I am.

Contents

Preface

I have spent a very significant portion of my adult life immersed in that tough and tender dialogue known as psychotherapy, first as a patient and then as a therapist (and at times as a patient once more). Again and again I have felt that at last I really knew what I was doing. And again and again I have returned to the feeling that I don't know what the hell it is all about. And then there are times when I feel that I *do* know something and that if I will only trust my feelings, then there is much that I do not need to understand, at least not in a way that requires that I be able to explain it all. Those are the best times.

At some points along the way, I have, several times, set out to write what I took to be distinctly separate books describing first, the person of the therapist, and next of the patient, and then the process of psychotherapy. But I find that an inner unity has emerged that relates each work to the others.

The primary aspect of this emergent relatedness expresses itself in that my first book, *Guru,* is a series of metaphors for a psychotherapist. Most of the reading that I have done about psychotherapy has made me feel either more certain or more bewildered. These states seem equally *un*useful to me. At first it seemed very strange to me that the readings that helped me most to trust what went on in my work as a psychotherapist were tales of Wizards and Shamans, of Hasidic Rabbis, Desert Monks, and Zen Masters. Not the materials of science and reason, but the stuff of poetry and myth instructed me best. So it was that I chose to write this book of metaphors.

My second book, *If You Meet the Buddha on the Road, Kill Him!,* consists of tales of the pilgrimage of psychotherapy patients. The guru instructs by metaphor and parable, but the pilgrim learns through the telling of his own tale. As a child, I was often so lonely and out of it that if I had not found the tales of others in the books I read, I believe I would have died. As a therapist, I am able to listen to the pilgrimage tales of my patients and to tell them my own, as we draw courage from each other along the way of our journey through the darkness. In every age men have set out on such pilgrimages. And so in my book (as in my work) I draw on earlier tales to light the way, from Gilgamesh, Chaucer, Dante and Shakespeare, to Conrad and Kafka.

My third work, *The Hanged Man*, describes the power of our meeting in psychotherapy, and the forces of darkness with which we must contend. Those dark forces which may guide or destroy us are most immediately available in dreams, as messages from the all-uniting dark soul. Just as *dreams* are the inner voice of humanity's most basic struggles, joys, ambiguities, so *myths* are its outer expression. The myth is everyone's story. And so, in this work, I have illuminated the recurring motifs of dreams and myths in the light of Jung's concept of the Archetypes, those timeless unconscious channels through which the dark waters of life have so long flowed.

Whatever inner unity my writings may display has been underscored by their setting in my private life. The forces of darkness and of light have further dramatized the one-ness of what must be by insinuating elements of the plot of my off-stage life into the performance of my work and the composition of my creative efforts.

During the writing of *Guru*, I underwent surgery for a brain tumor. My ordeal served as a backdrop for the creation of this manuscript, and the writing of it served as a therapeutic venture for me, a sort of thrust toward life. Throughout this struggle, my dialogue with the people with whom I work as a psychotherapist, dialogue expressive of my anguish and their own, drew us all closer together, making us more aware of what we had to offer each other as human beings. Early in my recuperation I took time out from the work on the book to write an account of my ordeal and of our dialogue. I have included it in *Guru* as an epilogue, both to make the book a more personal experience for the reader and to offer testimony to my own conception of the relationship between the contemporary guru and those to whom he would offer guidance.

The period during which I was writing *Buddha* was a time of anguish and craziness in my personal life. No longer able to sustain the overstanced denial and caricature of existential adventure of what I had titled the "growth experience" of my partially removed brain tumor, I crashed. The hidden sorrow and hurt of my helplessness before a painful present and a menacing future threw me into a deep and suicidal despair. I sought therapy once more as a patient. My therapist was a life-saving help, as were my family, my friends, and the people I was treating. They all supported and guided me through my mad scene.

And then, during the writing of *The Hanged Man,* my tumor grew once more and I underwent and survived another terrifying bout of brain surgery. Fortunately, there were no catastrophic consequences, but again it was not possible to remove the entire tumor. I must go on living with this time-bomb-with-no-clock in my head. It will grow again, and the ticket of admission for more time in my life is that of further pain and limitation. And during some future surgical ordeal, far sooner than I would choose, I will die. This too has become part of the scenario of my work with my patients, part of the drama of my writings.

But I feel content to enjoy what life is yet available to me as I can, being what I may with the people whom I love, and dying, as I have tried to live, *in my own way.* It should not surprise me that the working title of my next book is *This Side of Tragedy.*

For those of you particularly interested in the process of therapy I recommend *Back to One: A Practical Guide for Psychotherapists.* This book is a detailed description of how I do therapy. I offer it only as a guide. These are not the ways to work. They are simply my ways of working. They need not be yours, though some may suit your own path. I offer it to encourage you to become ever clearer about the fundamentals of your own style of work.

SBK

I *A Spiritual Guide for Each Age*

1 *Helpers, Healers, and Guides*

"In my craft and sullen art . . ."

—DYLAN THOMAS

It has always been true that, in seeking guidance, the many have depended on the few. In every time, in every place, there is always a "creative minority"[1] to whom others turn for leadership, for guidance, for courage, for understanding, for beauty. Answers may change. Only the questions remain eternal. These few who guide stand before the many, not as the ideal bearers of final truths, but simply as the *most extraordinarily human* members of the community.

Men differ, one from another, within each society. And certainly they differ even more radically from one culture to another. Yet certain aspects of the human situation remain common to us all. In the final analysis, perhaps we are all more alike than we are different.

Each person begins life helpless and in need of care, and must find his place in the family or the group on which he depends for survival. Each develops skills with which to cope with the physical environment and with other people. Each makes clear his identity as a child, only to be confronted with the many flowerings and sexual awakenings of puberty. Then comes the struggle through the adolescent changes from being a child to becoming an adult.

Grown-up roles and demands for achievement must be met. The pleasures and pains of courtships and marriage, the bearing, raising, and giving up of children, and the eventual decline of sexuality and vitality, all must be met. And finally, death must be faced—the death of loved ones and of enemies, and, at the center, the ever-present inevitability of one's own death.

In unspoken recognition of the turmoil that attends these crises, each culture provides institutions, rituals, and agents to help the individual through these transitions, to ease his passage. The psychotherapist is the contemporary Western agent for helping other men in the midst of such struggles or in the unhappiness that follows their failure to find satisfying resolutions to such common human crises.

3

A spiritual guide who helps others to move from one phase of their lives to another is sometimes called a "guru." He is a special sort of a teacher, a master of the rites of initiation. The guru appears to introduce his disciples to new experiences, to higher levels of spiritual understanding, to greater truths. Perhaps what he really does is to give them the freedom that comes with accepting their imperfect, finite human situation. For me, Sigmund Freud's most convincing statement of what a psychoanalyst could do for a patient was his saying: "No doubt fate would find it easier than I do to relieve you of your illness, but you will be able to convince yourself that much will be gained if we succeed in transforming your hysterical misery into common unhappiness."[2]

Whatever it is that the guru does bring, he may offer it in many different forms. He may be a magic healer, a spiritual guide, a teacher, a sage, or a prophet. All of these manifestations have in common that each chooses to act as an agent for positive change, for growth, for personal development. Each attempts to aid those suffering from evil, illness, ignorance, or possibly simply from youth. Each is effective to the extent that he is relevant to the needs of the time and place in which he appears.

The guru is able to pierce the vanity of the conventional wisdom of the group. He understands that reason and laws and customs of the moment offer only the illusion of certainty. The people may believe that what they are taught that "one must do" or "one must not do" constitutes something real. The guru can see that these formalities are no more than games. After he has passed among you, you will find that, "he sank beneath your wisdom like a stone."[3]

His is the language of prophecy, not of a fatalistically fixed future which can be predicted, but of an understanding of what man is like, of where man has been, and of where man is going. He knows that a man cannot escape himself without destroying himself. Only by facing his fears, at times with the help of the guru, can he become what he is and realize what he might.

It has always been clear in myths and fairy tales that to flee from a prophecy is to make it come true. So it was with Oedipus. Before he was born, his father Laius married Jocasta and was warned that he would perish at the hands of his own son. In order to escape the oracle's prophecy, Laius avoided Jocasta until he took her once while drinking to forget his lust. He ordered Jocasta to destroy the child at birth, but she felt she could not and so gave him to a servant who was to leave the infant Oedipus to die of exposure in the mountains. The baby was found by a shepherd of King Polybus of Corinth, and the king raised him as his own son.

When Oedipus had grown, he was afraid that he was illegitimate and went to the oracle to find out. The oracle prophesied that he would return home, murder his father, and marry his mother. Horrified by the prophecy, and knowing Corinth as his only home, Oedipus fled. It was, of course, on his journey of escape from the prophecy that he met and killed Laius (not knowing that this was his father) and later met and married Jocasta (not knowing that she was Laius' widow, nor that she was his own mother).

The guru, however he appears at different times and places, is always that member of the community who understands the "forgotten language"[4] of the myth and the dream. Myths are the folk wisdom of the world. They appear in every culture, and they retain their qualities of wonder centuries after they have arisen, in times and places in which men no longer "believe" in them. The reason for this is that they speak to fundamental human experiences, experiences which obtain for all men at all times.

If the myth is the outer expression of the human condition's basic struggles, joys, and ambiguities, then the dream is its inner voice. It may be that by the standards of any given set of social conventions, we are "less reasonable and less decent in our dreams but . . . we are also more intelligent, wiser, and capable of better judgment when we are asleep than when we are awake."[5]

This is the knowing-by-metaphor which the guru can teach us, the trusting of the intuitive. Here the dream is a man's best judgment, uncluttered by reason and convention. The way in which the guru understands the myth and the dream may be made clearer by contrasting this sort of understanding with the Freudian psychoanalytic understanding of the dream.

For Freud the dream (and the myth) was a means by which the individual could avoid disruption of sleep or peace. For example, if the alarm clock rings and we begin at that point to dream of church bells ringing in the distance, we clothe the irritating call to rising in a pleasant fancy from which we do not need to disturb our rest. Or if during the night, some upsetting impulse arises from our unconscious, we disguise it as a dream figure whom we need not recognize. Only if the disguise is not sufficient do we wake in terror from what we then recall as a nightmare.

The orthodox analyst may then help the patient, whose dreams he hears reported, to learn to interpret those dreams, to learn what universal symbols and what personal associations make up the dream. Bit by bit, the analyst and the patient can "translate" the dream. In contrast, the guru, if he is gifted, reads the story as anyone would who was bilingual. He does not translate—he understands. He teaches this direct understanding, this knowing how to think once more in the forgotten language of myths and dreams.

Among the best of the helpers, the healers, and the guides are those who can be described as "charismatic." To have charisma is to possess the gift of grace. The Greek origin of the word relates to the Graces of mythology, those lovely goddesses of talent who brought joy, brilliance, and beauty into the lives of men. Even today, charisma may still be defined as "a free gift or favour . . . a grace or talent."[6] Further shadings of meaning have since evolved, meanings that make clearer what it is to be a gifted guru.

The term *charisma* was given a religious significance when it appeared in the early Greek versions of the New Testament. There, when Paul speaks "concerning spiritual gifts,"[7] he is no longer talking in terms of Greek concerns with talents in music and in the arts. He is talking of such gifts from God as prophecy, understanding of the mysteries, the working of miracles, talking in tongues, and the gift of healing. But, Paul added, that which gives these gifts their meaning is not the mere wonder of them but how they are used to help other men. So it is that he says: "And though I have the gift of prophecy, and understand all mysteries, and all knowledge, and though I have all faith, so that I could remove mountains, and have not charity, I am nothing."[8]

It is not enough then that a guru be a gifted magician. His talents must not be used merely as a celebration of his powers, no matter how remarkable. His gifts find meaning only as they are used in the service of offering an opportunity to another. Otherwise he "speaketh not unto men, but (only) unto God."[9]

Max Weber introduced a sociological meaning to the concept when he developed his "value-neutral" image of such extraordinary men. He delineated three bases for the authority underlying leadership in a community.[10] These included Traditional, characterized by "patri-archal . . . domination"; Bureaucratic, a legalistic defining of authority; and finally, Charismatic.

Charismatic leadership always stands over against the other two bases, as it is "strange to all rule and tradition."[11] The charismatic leader comes to power as one to whom others submit because of their belief in his extraordinary personal gifts. He may be a prophet, a shaman, a magical sorcerer, or even a leader of hunting expeditions.*

*Full bibliographical information appears in the Chapter Notes, p. 167.

His followers are committed to belief in his having qualities far beyond those of other men, qualities that in the past were valued as being supernatural.

It does not matter whether these extraordinary personal qualities of the charismatic leader are actual, alleged, or presumed. Such a leader arises when the people need him, at a time when the old order is to be challenged, when he has reason to stand in opposition to the traditional powers. This occurs, as I see it, at a time when the established order is suppressing fundamental human spiritual qualities in the people whom it was originally set up to serve. He sets "his personal charisma against the dignity consecrated by tradition in order to break their power or force them into his service."[12]

He may, like Jesus, come to restore the law, but he does so by overturning it with revolutionary reinterpretation. Remember that in the Sermon on the Mount, Jesus reminded the people: "Think not that I am come to destroy the law. . . ."[13] Yet every time he invoked the law by saying, "Ye have heard that it was said by them of old time . . .,"[14] he would end up changing the law with his invocations of, "But I say unto you. . . ."[15]

According to Max Weber, charismatic leaders appear at times of social change. Their followers support them with a "devotion born of distress and enthusiasm."[16] I do not, therefore, suggest that all gifted gurus also play the role of revolutionary social leader. Yet, perhaps each in his own way can help to free the people whom he guides. He can liberate them from taking seriously the legalistic games of bureaucratic conventions. He can also help them to see that the patriarchal domination of traditionalism need not bind a grown man.

It is, indeed, the guru's own freedom that inspires others to be free and may point the way. One of the sources of charisma has been described as lying in "the apparent unpredictability of the leader's behavior and his seeming indifference to the most awesome obstacles and dangers. This combination of unpredictable arbitrariness with naïve fearlessness is very similar to the innocent spontaneity of the child. . . ."[17]

In my own experience with the gifted gurus of psychotherapy, the charismatic ones, such impressions are frequent. It seems to me that the central quality in this spontaneity is that such a man trusts himself. It is not so much that he is responding in ways which are beyond other men (or lesser therapists). Rather it seems that he is past worrying about how he is doing. No longer expecting to be unafraid or certain or perfect, he gives himself over to being just as he is at the moment. He accepts his fear, lives with his uncertainty, finds his imperfection sufficient.

Unconcerned with being more than he is at any given moment
and satisfied to be able to do what he can, he is able to do far more
than he could if he were still distracted by the question of how well
he was doing. Of course, disciples of such a gifted guru will at first
be awed by the difference between his seeming confidence and power,
on the one hand, and their own helplessness and inadequacy, on
the other. The guru then tries to help his follower to see that there
is no difference between them, except as the follower diminishes
himself to give the power to the guru. The follower maintains the
imbalance to avoid the awful responsibility of being equal to everyone
else in the world and completely on his own, while retaining the
hope that the guru will take care of him. To maintain his own freedom,
the guru must try to free the disciple from himself.

Some fear that charismatic leadership may be deceptively manipulative and ultimately impersonal and authoritarian. They see the charismatic follower as always having a dependent security orientation, born
of never-to-be-resolved identification with the leader and ending in
the blind and hopeless devotion of someone who will never be free.

Of course, any form of personal power is subject to abuse. The
trust of others is a responsibility just because there is a temptation
to exploit it. Some gurus are corrupt, and those that are not may
become corrupt. In time any form of help that works, ultimately does
become corrupt. Each type of guru can only be effective for a time
within a given setting. The success of every kind of gifted guru inevitably contains within it the seeds of its own failure. Like Dylan Thomas's
"oak . . . felled in the acorn,"[18] each beginning already implies movement toward an ending. Decay is the other face of growth.

Just to the extent that any particular guru is helpful, to that same
extent are his efforts open to the processes of corruption. In many
instances it may be true that to become a guru, a man must overcome
his minor vices and lesser lusts. But at the same time it may be that
to be a guru in itself requires that he live with the greatest of all
lusts, the continuing temptation to arrogance. And if a particular guru
is not himself corrupted, then surely his success will prove too great
a burden for those who succeed him in whatever form of spiritual
leadership he has embodied.

There are many sources of corruption which threaten the successful
guru and the disciples who take his place. Among others these include
the possibility of becoming institutionalized within the larger society,
of being deified by his own followers, or of being tempted to self-
elevation by his own arrogance. The meanings that the guru has
brought to his followers may be diluted by empty ritualistic imitation.

His metaphors may be reified by those who inherit his mantle in succeeding generations, thus extending the form of his teachings without continuing their substance.

Yet, nothing else lasts. Why, then, should we expect more of those to whom we turn for guidance than we are capable of ourselves? In this ambiguous world, made up as it is of moments, fragments, bits, and pieces, we must learn to take love where we find it. And then we must learn to grieve its passing so that we may make room for the next moment.

2 Training Today's Guru

". . . all the deadly virtues."

—DYLAN THOMAS

Once we understand that a guru is by no means simply a highly skilled technician, how then can we train one? To be a guru is to have grace of manner, powerful personal presence, a spirit of inner freedom, and an inspirationally creative imagination. How are we to teach such qualities, and how are they to be learned? What will this all mean for the contemporary guru? What of today's psychotherapist, whether psychiatrist, clinical psychologist, psychiatric social worker, or pastoral counseling minister? Presently, the goal of their respective educational preparations is "to impart specialized expert training [rather than] to awaken charisma, . . . heroic qualities or magical gifts."[1]

Let us consider the current routes open to those who would offer personal guidance to troubled people. In our time, such guidance often goes under the name of psychotherapy. The formal routes to its practice are various kinds of graduate training prescribed by certain kinds of professional schools.

If a young man aspires to that sort of guruship that has the highest social status and is likely to guarantee the greatest financial return, he must attend medical school. There he will become a "doctor," a healer of "patients" who suffer from "mental illness." One would hope that his subsequent psychiatric residence would be of help in moving him past being a curer of diseases. Such specialized training might be expected to turn him toward accepting himself as one struggling human being who will be open to experiencing the struggles of another.

Unfortunately, this is not usually the case. Instead, his clinical impersonality is supported by the impossible task of having to treat too many people in too little time within the deadening confines of the monolithic, managerial institution of the mental hospital. He will emerge being called a "psychiatrist," but he will have to find some other road to enlightenment if he is to be able to overcome the benign-ly domineering attitudes engendered by his professional training.

Another choice open to an aspiring guru might be to work toward obtaining a Ph.D. in clinical psychology. This course is not likely to end up paying quite as much or having as much social prestige, but it is presented as being a more purely scientific venture than is the study of medicine.

The actual training of the clinical psychologist often puts a premium on an attitude of scientific detachment, on an interest in theorizing in terms of abstract models of what human behavior is all about, and on putting objective clinical instruments (tests) between the psychologist and the subject. The clinical psychologist, too, must find a way of overcoming his education if he is ever to be able to help other people to find themselves and to solve their personal problems.

A third alternative for the would-be guru is the profession of psychiatric social work. The training of social workers aims at turning out professionals who are geared toward ameliorating social problems, who will purport to "speak for the voiceless." Yet social work comes, in part, out of the controlling, aristocratic tradition of the Lady Bountiful and too often ends up as a form of governmental agency administration of cases. Social workers are being trained to "enable" clients to achieve their own desires, but the training includes "placements" in agencies whose structure, coupled with the press of too many cases, too often leads the social worker to have to "decide what is best" for the client.

It is true that there are clear and dependable lines of supervision in social casework training and practice. Nonetheless, psychiatric social workers are often differently, but no better, prepared to do psychotherapy when they finish their training than are psychiatrists or clinical psychologists when they complete theirs.

Those who seek the position of guru by way of seminary training in the ministry are in a somewhat different position than these other three therapeutic professions. For one thing, many ministers who end up doing psychotherapy get to that point because of growing dissatisfaction with enduring the hopelessness and helplessness that they experience in parish work.

Their training for parish ministry, diverse as it is, still fosters some traditional ministerial attitudes, ways of feeling and of acting which are antithetical to the successful performance of the therapeutic role. Ministers' thrust toward saving souls inclines them to conduct rescue operations that do not facilitate growth in the emotionally troubled people whom they set out to help. Being helpful, in itself, rather than simply being with the other person in hope of his having a useful experience, can result in setting goals for him that he must set for himself. There is also much pressure on the minister to be "good," which too often results in denial of evil in himself, insistence on being "unselfish," and an unwillingness to fight openly for what he wants. While his training fosters concern for the troubled and a willingness to give of himself, it limits his capacity to offer a model of self-acceptance and freedom of expression to those he would counsel.

These men often turn to the old/new profession of pastoral counseling with a sense of the rot and the irrelevance of the contemporary social institution of the church. They may even play out their new roles within the context of private practice, but they work in a shadowy borderland, sometimes denying it is psychotherapy they are practicing, humbly owning up to nothing more competitively professional than "counseling."

Upon examination, their attitudes about their work turn out to be a confused and confusing amalgam. They defer to the "medical judgments" of the psychiatrists. Yet they turn out to believe, secretly, that only they, the Pastoral Counselors, participate in truly profound engagements with clients, patients, or troubled souls; only they can deal with matters of "ultimate concern."

Like the psychiatrist, the clinical psychologist, and the psychiatric social worker, the minister must not only survive his training but also transcend it, if he is to become a responsible spiritual guide who knows what he is doing. The minister, too, must find some way to be illumined, to unlearn what he has been taught, and to learn that which cannot simply be taught.

Each has taken a different path toward the common goal of being in a position to help others to grow, to be whole, to be free. Yet each finds that choosing a specific path means undergoing some particular set of prescribed training experiences. These varied trainings are required to obtain the credentials which are demanded by the law or by tradition before he is permitted to try to help others. Training leads to the union card of the particular trade under whose guise he may become a guru, the union card of the M.D., the Ph.D., the M.S.W., or the B.D.

Ironically, for each it is the very training designed to equip him that handicaps him most when he tries to be an authentic personal guide for another. Psychiatric training breeds a clinical, managerial attitude toward "patients." Clinical Psychology encourages an objective, detached examination of "subjects." Psychiatric Social Workers too often end up becoming sentimental and patronizing toward the "cases" whose troubled lives they once sought to ease. Finally, seminaries tend to turn out too many clergymen who would sacrifice themselves to save the "lost souls" whom they are to shepherd.

What then is a man to do? If he wishes to be of personal help to other troubled men, the main channels now open to him are psychiatry, clinical psychology, psychiatric social work, and the ministry. Each of these ways will lead to the opportunity to take on the role of personal helper, but paradoxically, each will develop attitudes that will limit his capacity to fulfill that role.

So it is that the most important aspects of the development of a psychotherapist occur outside the context of his professional school training, having more to do with his own personal sufferings, pleasures, risks, and adventures. In solitude, and later in the company of one who is already a guru, he must struggle with his own demons and must dare to free himself of them.

For a contemporary psychotherapist, such events must take place in a number of different settings. He must struggle alone, as well as in the company of significant others, with the joys and the agonies of his own personal life. As a patient in his own therapy experience, he must work out with *his* therapist the ways in which he binds himself. When he begins to take on the role of therapist to his own early patients, he must undergo supervision. Here he will not simply learn techniques, but will encounter the supervisor in a way so open and intimate that he will never forget what it was like. This experience will turn him toward the personal presence of his own supervised patients so that from then on, it will be very hard for him not to remember to remember that there is nobody here but us people.

Psychotherapy is merely today's name for an activity that has been going on among men since someone first discovered that one man could care enough about the suffering of another that he would be willing to open himself to the agony of the other in order to try to be of aid and comfort. The nature of the efforts to help which have followed from this are as ambiguous and as exciting as a kaleidoscope. This freely-living, ever-changing, never-changing condition of one man putting himself in the place of him-who-would-help-and-guide-another is threatened with imprisonment by the oppressive modern ideals of progress and objective certainty.

Freudian Psychoanalysis taught us much about the unknown motives which guide men's actions. It promised to explain everything and ended up explaining everything *away*. The hollow myths of psychoanalysis tell us that all of our treasured accomplishments are nothing more than sublimations of unacceptable infantile urges. Psychoanalysis has taught us that the real meaning of our lives has little to do with the ways in which we experience ourselves in the world. Instead, such things are only known to those initiated in reading the symbols of the Unconscious, which are rooted deeply in the past.

Psychoanalysis has been satirically described as a situation in which the psychoanalyst is always one-up on the patient. Many maneuvers, both crude and subtle, are required to maintain this reciprocity of superior and inferior positions. By definition, the interplay is one in which "the patient insists that the analyst be one-up while desperately trying to put him one-down, and the analyst insists that the patient remain one-down in order to help him to learn to become one-up."[2]

This balance is first established by the patient's voluntarily seeking out the analyst's help, coming to see him at the analyst's convenience, and paying him a great deal of money. The patient must lie supine on a couch while the analyst is free to sit, above, so to speak, and behind him, where he can watch without being observed by the patient. The patient must say anything that comes to mind, no matter how seemingly irrational, inappropriate, or gross. The analyst needs to say nothing, and usually does.

What is more, they agree that the patient does not really know what he is talking about, that he is motivated by unconscious drives, and that the analyst knows more about such matters than does the patient. The analyst's reactions to the patient are "interpretations," or truths. The patient's responses to the analyst, by unflattering contrast, are bits of "transference," or fantasies. Obviously, there is only one way for the patient to redress this one-up/one-down imbalance. The sane, mature response would be to get up off the couch, walk out, slam the door, and never return. This takes five years to come about. It is called a cure.

In addition to Psychoanalysis, there is a second contemporary approach to helping people with their personal problems. This is the method of Behavior Therapy, a way of dealing with people in scientific terms within which human behavior is thought of as lawful, predictable, and controllable. Whatever help this approach has offered in changing limited, often intractable, behavior problems (such as bedwetting) must be measured against the danger of having scientific managers programming us to behave predictably in ways that will be best for all.

Their claim to moral and political neutrality becomes, in effect, a means of diverting attention from glaring social evils, and they are in fact used—*or would be if they worked*—for warfare and social engineering, manipulation of people for the political economic purposes of the powers that be.[3]

In the face of all of this, one might well wonder what becomes of the personal relationship between the helper and the helped, the relationship that mediates the impact of the guru of Behavior Therapy, on his disciple. The image becomes clear when described by one of its advocates: "The therapist, as the central variable in the therapeutic situation, is *a social 'reinforcement machine,'* programed [sic] by prior training and experience . . . to influence the probability of selected behavior change in the patient."[4]

There is a viable alternative to the patronizing esotericism of Psychoanalysis, on the one hand, and the dehumanizing programming of Behavior Therapy on the other. This alternative is the "Third Force," Humanistic Psychology. This Third Force is made up of gurus who are unwilling to sacrifice what they consider to be fundamentally human. They will not make offerings either at the Freudian altar of psychopathology or at the Behavioristic temple of science.

Humanistic Psychologists answer Psychoanalysis by foregoing head-shrinking for mind-expanding. Their response to the Behavior Therapists is a refusal to accept the seeming certainty of a computerized canning of life, instead choosing liberation over automation. The Third Force has reclaimed human values that the other two approaches tend to ignore or to reduce, concerns such as authenticity, imagination, love, and joy.

The guru of the Third Force, the Humanistic Therapist, meets the man he tries to help as one risking human being to another. One therapist with such a personal thrust to his work has described the adventure of therapy in this wonderful way:

I imply to those with whom I sit that I am like a safety net. They may dare risk tiptoeing themselves out upon that tight-wire over the unknown and be reassured that even, if their terror slips them and they plummet downward, all they will suffer is a rubberball bouncing until they can right themselves again. But what of me? As I give up each worn-out piece of technique and venture forth to discover the limits of myself and therapy, the other person may be shocked to find me approaching him at those heights from the other end of the wire. At those times we may both wonder: "Who is tending the net?"[5]

Psychoanalysis and Behavior Therapy are but temporary misconceptions in the history of man's quest for the illusion of everlasting certainty in a life that is ephemeral and in a world that is ultimately

ambiguous. The Psychoanalyst and the Behavior Therapist have appeared only recently upon the scene as today's gurus. Or perhaps
by now it is somewhat late in the day for the Psychoanalyst, rather
well into the evening. Only for the Humanistic Psychologist is it still
dawn. But he assured, his twilight will also come.

3 Illumination by Metaphor

"... man be my metaphor."

—DYLAN THOMAS

The old, old philosophical question, "How do we know?" has been answered in terms of three basic ways of knowing: We can know things *rationally*, by thinking about them. If they seem logically consistent within themselves and with what else we know, we accept them as being true. We do not believe that they are true if they seem illogical. A second way of knowing is deciding matters *empirically*. In this case, we depend upon our senses, truth being a matter of perceiving correctly. We can check out these experiences by objective experiments. The third way is knowing *metaphorically*. In this mode we do not depend primarily on thinking logically nor on checking our perceptions. Understanding the world metaphorically means we depend on an intuitive grasp of situations, in which we are open to the symbolic dimensions of experience, open to the multiple meanings that may all coexist, giving extra shades of meaning to each other.

Of course, we all use all three basic ways of knowing in making our way through the uncertainties we come upon. Yet in our time knowing metaphorically is much neglected. "Because of twentieth-century encapsulation within the epistemology of empiricism, contemporary man finds it difficult to be open to symbolic and intuitive cognition."[1] It would be fruitful here to pause to consider just what is meant by the term *metaphor*, what purpose is served by speaking metaphorically, and what special relevance metaphors might have to the understanding of what it means to be a guru.

Generally, a metaphor is defined as a way of speaking in which one thing is expressed in terms of another, whereby this bringing together throws new light on the character of what is being described. The simplest examples would be such statements as: "Mary is an angel," or "John has the heart of a lion." Technical distinctions can be made between the metaphor and other comparative figures of speech such as similes and analogies. However, for our purposes,

17

we will "take metaphor in the broad sense, as denoting any kind of comparison as a basis for the kind of illumination we call poetic."[2]

Of course, the use of metaphors is by no means restricted to the intentional writing of poetry. Such figures of speech may be used simply for the sake of expressing something more vividly, more clearly, or more memorably. Metaphor may indeed be the most natural mode in some instances. For example: "[in] the infant's mind . . . everything soft is a mother; everything that meets his reach is food. Being dropped, even into bed, is terror itself. . . . Children mix dream and reality . . . every symbol has to do metaphorical as well as literal duty."[3]

In primitive societies as well, metaphor may be the mode. For such people the sun may be the source of warmth and life. Therefore they understand that God is the sun and that the sun is God. Let us not be superior about such matters without remembering that in twentieth-century America some people partake of wine and wafer that is the body and blood of Christ. If you insist that religion is always the last bastion of the primitive, remember too that you can go to jail for desecrating the American flag, because the flag is the country.

Even sophisticated, "enlightened" scientists find metaphor a useful way of formulating and solving problems. "Biologists postulate a genetic code, implying that the organic seeds of human life share the features of some secret communication system (which can then be decoded and understood)."[4]

Support for the idea that metaphor is a fundamental aspect of human experience is not restricted to the responses found in infants and in primitives. "Metaphor is the law of growth of every semantic. It is not a development, but a principle. . . . the lowest, completely unintentional products of the human brain are madly metaphorical fantasies, that often make no literal sense whatever: I mean the riotous symbolism of dreams."[5]

Beginning with "pictures in the head,"[6] perhaps all thinking may be said to have some metaphoric aspects, metaphor being "the source of all generality."[7] And one experiences a note of truth in the contention that "genuinely new ideas . . . usually have to break in upon the mind through some great and bewildering metaphor."[8]

In all of this, I would like to be careful not to turn away from the use of metaphor that is genuinely, intentionally, and creatively poetic. Happy as I am that metaphor "makes life an adventure in understanding"[9] for us all, I am particularly grateful to those poets who use it to tune my ears, to bring new light to my eyes, to reawaken my soul. This chapter begins with a quote from that Welsh singer of words, Dylan Thomas. He speaks a central truth for all of his poetry when he says, "Man be my metaphor,"[10] for it is in terms of the fundamental human concerns that he wrote. He created music and destroyed himself. Dylan is Mankind.

His most basic themes were the great polarities: birth and death, sex and violence, growth and decay. In a wonderful funny/sad, lusty/bitter poem entitled "Lament,"[11] an outrageously ribald satyr, now grown old, tells of his life, describing it with irony, gusto, and black humor. This "old ram rod," now "a black sheep with a crumpled horn," is "dying of women . . . dying of bitches . . . dying of strangers."

At the other end of the spectrum, Dylan can offer a metaphor so tender that we can love a bit more gently for having come upon it. Such a one is his description of truant youngsters at play: "the wild boys innocent as strawberries."[12]

Long ago, Paracelsus wrote that a guru should not tell "the naked truth. He should use images, allegories, figures, wonderous [sic] speech, or other hidden roundabout ways."[13] This is still good advice. It is true that metaphor "orients the mind toward freedom and novelty . . . encourages . . . daring . . . [and] pure joy."[14] But more than that, metaphor offers a kind of vision and truth not open to computer-bank reduction.

In order to be certain and to be "scientific," modern psychology has thrown away much of the wisdom of thousands of years of men's struggle to understand themselves, to be with one another, to find meaning in their lives. It has denied the immediacy of each man's experience, his encounter with metaphor, and reduced beyond recognition the concerns that make man most human. Modern psychology has lost the vision of life and growth to preoccupation with psychopathology and conditioned responses.

Some men would return us to ourselves and take us beyond. Who is to guide us on this journey? Who will be the new guru? We cannot go further in this search without a return to metaphor, without a recommitment to intuitive, subjective experience. It may not be measurable, but it is the measure of our humanity. We must transform our way of thinking about problems, our very way of perceiving and sensing things, if need be. The change we need is "the change from imitation to expression, and from the mirror to . . . the lamp."[15] By including our personal selves once more, we will come upon the world, and upon ourselves and each other, like explorers in a new land. Wonder will be upon us once more, and we must live with it "until the world become a human event."[16]

II *An Enchantment of Metaphors*

4 Metaphors from Primitive Religion

THE WITCH DOCTOR

Primitive people know that if there is evil or suffering present, it is because someone has brought it about. Something does not come out of nothing. *Cause* is an impersonal concept of modern man. *Blame* is the more basic experience of those who can see that something has gone wrong. When a crop fails, or a hunt goes badly, or someone mysteriously sickens and dies, it is time to find out who has done this bad magic. It is at such a time that the people of the tribe must turn to the Witch Doctor for help.

The bad thing has been brought about by the spirits or by ancestral shades, by male sorcerers or female witches. It is not without reason that these powerful beings bring on such misfortunes. Sometimes it is because someone has not followed the tribal rituals as he should, or perhaps another has not offered sufficient sacrifices at the village shrines. If so, those with the power to bewitch have cast a spell upon him as punishment for his negligence. These spells may range from the terrible loss of a newborn child to frighteningly troubled dreams, or even to simple stomachaches. The tribesman believes that such magical calamities, whether great or small, can only be set to rest by the counter-magic of the Witch Doctor.

Among the Ndembu tribesmen[1] of southern Africa, the Witch Doctor is a ritual specialist called the *chimbuki*. For these people all severe or persistent illness has a social explanation. When the powers of witchcraft are afoot, it is not only in response to the breach of ritual or custom. Dead ancestors may also punish living relatives "because kin are not living well together." Social conflict among the thirty or so men, women, and children who make up a village threatens the whole fabric of group life. Hidden grudges, secret jealousies and resentments may be met with harsh punishments by the ancestral shades. Anyone involved may be made a scapegoat for the group and afflicted with a punishment suited more to the extent of the quarreling in the village than to the extent to which he himself is actually at fault. At that point the task of the Witch Doctor is to magically divine the causes of the trouble in such a way as to bring to light the hidden struggles between tribesmen or among tribal factions.

Among the Ndembu tribesmen all of this gets worked out in the context of the Ihamba cult. The *ihamba* itself is an upper central incisor tooth of a deceased hunter, a fetish that serves as a central symbolic element in a complex system of beliefs and rituals. These teeth contain the hunter's power to kill animals, are removed at death, and inherited by appropriate relatives. At times of trouble, when spells are cast, the *ihamba*s of ancestral shades afflict victims by biting, eating, or sucking on them, by "going after meat." The victim falls ill, suffers pain, and may even die.

The experienced Witch Doctor, when called to divine (or diagnose) the witchcraft at work, begins by familiarizing himself with all the kin relationships and factional disputes in the village to which he is called. He learns from the gossip of travelers, as well as from assistants who act as spies and informants, of the nature of the victim's relationship to the headman and of the relevant family lineages. Next he may tactfully question everyone involved about the attitudes and relationships which constitute the social matrix in which the victim lives. Some will, of course, try to mislead him with false information, and he must see through such devices.

Next the Witch Doctor gathers secret medicines in a prescribed manner and brings forth cupping horns with which to withdraw the phantom *ihamba* from the victim's body. The tribe gathers for the ceremony; the medicines are administered, the cupping horns attached to the victim's body, and the drumming and singing begin. All who are present join in. Unfortunately, the first efforts are unsuccessful; the cupping horns do not immediately make the *ihamba* come out.

The Witch Doctor explains this to the assembled group in a way which reveals an elaborate account of the patient's life story and a salient description of the intra-tribal relationships. In order to make the *ihamba* come quickly, he requires that each member of the tribe come forward before the hunter's shrine and confess to all resentments and grudges which he may harbor toward the patient. It is necessary that each must "make his liver white," must purify his intentions toward the victim of witchcraft, or the tooth will "not allow itself to be caught." Finally the patient, as well, must come forward and acknowledge any bitterness he may harbor toward his fellow villagers.

All of this goes on for hours in a stop-start rhythm, which moves the whole group toward wanting nothing so much as to free itself from the spell, no matter what must be confessed to or given up. Finally the cupping horns are attached once more. The singing and dancing build in intensity to the thrust of the insistent drumming until, at last, the ancestral *ihamba*, the trouble-making tooth, is magically extracted.

This is, of course, big magic. The Witch Doctor himself is a reputable man and chief enemy of the witches. But in order to overcome witches, he must have a comparable power, dedicated to the well-being of the people. His understanding of the complex interactions of tribal life is, of course, a power he may be tempted to misuse; and if he gives way to using this power on an enemy, he becomes a witch himself.

The roots of most present-day remnants of the original healers of primitive religions are to be found among Priests or Shamans, or some later amalgam of the two. It is best that we look carefully at how it all began.

THE PRIEST AND THE SHAMAN

The dragon "Thou Shalt" . . . the social fiction of the moral law, has been slain by the lion of self-discovery; and the master roars . . . the lion roar; the roar of the great Shaman of the mountain peaks, of the void beyond all horizons, and of the bottomless abyss.[2]

Before man knew God, there were Shamans. With God came His Priests. This distinction between the Shaman and the Priest arose in man's earliest efforts to band together for survival and may still be found within remaining primitive cultures. The earliest spiritual guide, the Shaman, is the central helper-healer in the hunting and gathering societies. These include the paleolithic, stone-age hunting bands as well as their contemporary progeny, such as the Eskimo and the Crow Indian. The advent of the Priest as spiritual leader came later when men of the neolithic era settled into more stable planting societies. Examples of these primitive agricultural groups may still be found in the Hopi, Zuñi, and other pueblo-dwelling Indians. The culture of the planters is, of course, the basic model for modern civilizations as well. We may well have both gained and lost in the transition from the paradigm of the hunter to that of the planter.

Before we can understand the implications of the difference between shamanistic and priestly leadership, we must first examine what it meant to live in the cultures within which each arose. The hunters lived in small, loosely organized, mobile bands, often in communities of no more than twenty to thirty people. No one place could provide a long-term supply of the game and edible plants on which they lived. Permanent homes, abundant possessions, and elaborate social order were luxuries they could not afford as they kept on the move to track and kill game, forage for wild plants, and conduct episodic guerrilla warfare with rival hunting bands.

With the appearance of an agricultural economy came a kind of settling in. For the planters, it was necessary to live in one place and possible to survive in ever larger groups. Both the increase in social complexity and the need to live in tune with the seasons led to a more ordered life. It became possible to store food and to live in a more predictable world. It was a time to multiply possessions and to build a home in which to keep them. The people began to develop an elaborate social order to preserve what they had.

In the less predictable, more dangerous and fast-moving life of the hunter, the most important virtues had been self-reliance, personal initiative, imagination, and daring. It was this setting which spawned the Shaman as its spiritual leader, its healer, its helper, and its guide. Like the young people of today who are on their own "trips," the young Shaman-to-be was seen as a misfit; and like his contemporary counterparts, the singularity and depth of his own inner experiences served as the basis for his emerging capacity for inspired leadership. The Shaman has been characterized as follows: (1) he demonstrates a strange, nervous irritability from an early age; (2) he often seems to be "possessed" by spirits (usually described in ways suggesting hallucinations, trances, phobias, and seizures); (3) he withdraws into the solitude of the woods or the tundra to fast and meditate; (4) he "dies" and his soul journeys through the underworld of the land of spirits, during which time spiritual beings announce his coming shamanhood and teach him how to shamanize; (5) he finally returns reborn to the land of the living, to the community whom he now turns on with his visions and heals with the powers learned in healing himself, and whom he tries to get to explore what is in their own heads.[3]

In contrast to the hunters' need for daring and imagination, the planters' survival came to depend upon stability, order, and the sacrifice of individuality and self-determination for the greater good of the group. In return, the group would take care of some of the needs of the planter, needs which a hunter would have had to manage for himself. More and more, individual planters could become specialists, developing particular talents at the expense of more general competence.

With the focus on agriculture, the planters had to pay increased attention to the order of the natural world on which the crops seemed to depend. The rising and the setting of the sun, the waxing and the waning of the moon, the predictably changing seasons and the unpredictably changing weather, the constant stars and the inconstant ones (that is, the planets)—all of this spoke of an order to the universe, on which men relied and which they hoped to learn to control. One way to do this was to create a microcosmic social order that would fit in appeasing harmony with the macrocosm of nature.

It was in this context that the priesthood arose, an office aimed at establishing an intermediary who could deal with the gods who ruled the world. The Priest was ceremonially trained and raised above his fellow men, because he was the keeper of the rituals and administrator of the activities of the cult. Chief among the Priest's duties was to compel or persuade people to give up their commitment to their own personal interests, to their intuitive responses, to the immediacy of their own experiences; in short, their commitment to themselves. The Priest bade them sacrifice the very concerns which the Shaman attempted to inspire. Instead, the planters were to learn to identify themselves with the needs and the feelings of the group, with that which operated in the public domain and was sustained by authority and consensus.

The day of the hunter was past, and the Shaman's influence was restricted accordingly. "Victory of a socially anointed priesthood over the highly dangerous and unpredictable force of individual endowment"[4] was the wave of the future. The way of the plants was to be learned. The individual person was to be no more than the single grain of wheat, an expendable sacrifice for the good of the whole crop, for the survival of the order of the social group.

Among the hunters there had seemed to be no virtue in patient submission to the group. They had lived, not in a unified world run by gods, but in a wild place populated by free-roaming spirits and wandering men. In each beast to be killed, there lived a powerful spirit, which had to be overcome. In such a world there was no priesthood born of ritual and tradition, no servant of God and suppressor of men. In his stead there stood the Shaman, risen to the position of spiritual guide by virtue of the power of his own inner struggles and the impact of his own compelling visions. His task was to render the spirits subservient to himself and to free ordinary men to experience the vision of their own inner being. The Priest qualified by learning ritual acts and words verbatim, while the Shaman was required to demonstrate a talent for improvisation, for creative adaptation to new situations.

These differing values were reflected in the puberty rites as well. These rites were aimed at fostering the virtues that defined manhood in each group. In the primitive planting societies, when a boy came of age, he was taken off to the men's compound and put through an ordeal of ritual sacrifice. It was the same for each boy—some specified tattooing, scarring, or circumcision carried out in a prescribed manner along with the reciting of traditional prayers. Up to this point, the boy had been taught to believe some allegorical tales used to deceive women and children. This would be equivalent to the far less systematic telling of the myth of the stork, used in recent times to screen children from mysteries of conception and birth. During the puberty rites the youth would be let in on the "real truth" about the meaning of life, the nature of God, and the mission of men. All of the tribal secrets were disclosed to him so that *he might come to be the same as all other men.*

In contrast to the elaborate ceremonies and group ecstasies of the planters' initiatory rites, the hunter's transition from boyhood to manhood was stark and individual. Typically, as among the Ojibwa, an American Indian hunting tribe, when it came time, a father led his son out into the woods to leave him to fast, to be alone, and to ponder the meaning of his life. As it was to be a time of self-discovery, the boy was not told what he might expect to encounter. No socially approved image was offered to him. Rather, he was given the understanding that he would have a vision, his own vision of whom he was to be and what he was to do with his life. He was told that whatever this vision was, whatever he learned about himself and the world, should be trusted and accepted. When he returned, his vision would be honored by the tribe, *simply because it was his own and because he had discovered it for himself.*

How, then, does the Shaman-to-be differ from these other struggling youths? It seems, on the one hand, that he is more deeply vulnerable to his own inner turmoil, less able to resolve it in communion with others, and more courageous in plunging into the very depths of his being to find what lies at the heart of it. The Shaman is that man of all the hunters who has the greatest, the most compelling, the most powerful personal vision. His vision is so fulfilling that no group can face down a Shaman. He can stand alone if need be. He begins by having to resolve a crucial inner struggle, a crisis in his own identity that is of monumental proportion, a matter of life or death. Although the Shaman is then said to be wrestling with the spirits, it is not spiritual beings outside of himself with whom he must struggle, but his own thoughts, ideas, feelings, manifestations of his own inner turmoil.

A young man who is a potential Shaman begins by being viewed by the community as a "sick" man, caught as he is in an overpowering psychological crisis, expressed as deep mental confusion and even as physical illness. If he can cure himself, he is then led to shamanize, that is, to cure others as a matter of his own personal survival. His choices are limited. He must shamanize, go mad, or die. His own successful battle with the spirit world endows him with a depth, a sensitivity, an intuitive knowledge which empowers him to help others. And his own self-healing process must be renewed again and again throughout his life.

The emotional and spiritual crisis which the Shaman-to-be undergoes is an experience of death and rebirth. He may view the ordeal as being dragged off, consumed, and reconstructed by spirits; taken into the bowels of the earth or deep beneath the waters; or torn apart by animals and coming together bit by bit. The imagery in which this struggle is expressed will be shaped and colored by his local environs, in a creative attempt to speak concretely of his journey to the heart of the world, into the pit of his own soul. Thus a Greenlander is swallowed by a bear; a Siberian is cut into pieces, boiled, and eaten, later to be hatched out in a bird's egg; an Australian is pierced by a spear in a cave, etc. Each expresses his descent and re-emergence in a way befitting his own culture.

The description of events at each stage of his struggle "appear in the form of metaphors, as outward events, whereas they are, of course, inner events."[5] These psychological experiences take place while the Shaman is in a state of trance, in which he voluntarily gives himself over to the journey to the underworld. Yet these experiences are always described in terms of images from the real world. Later the events are remembered as miracles which actually took place. Every transformation, like any loss of the old to gain the new, involves terrible pain. The novice must undergo several such transformations in order to at last become a powerful Shaman. After years of such a chain of experiences, a breakthrough of illumination can occur through which the aspirant emerges as a full-fledged Shaman.

This transformation occurs with the aid of helping spirits, dream figures who show him the way and teach him how to shamanize. An older Shaman may take part in his initiation, but usually in the role of guide and enabler rather than instructor. It is through his own visions that the aspiring Shaman must become illuminated, and from them that he must draw his increased psychic powers.

These new powers appear to be transmitted to other people whom he tries to help; or, more likely, he arouses similar powers in them. The Shaman offers much in the way of healing and guidance, and he can bring spiritual calm and confidence to the tribe by helping them to draw on each of their own personal visions. But hunters are tough-minded, and he may have to use the trickery of a preliminary magic show in order to command their attention and to engage the group manipulatively in what will become an experience of total commitment on both sides. This trickery will "consist principally in the ability to hide about his person and to produce at will small quartz pebbles and bits of stick; and, of hardly less importance than this sleight of hand, the power of looking preternaturally solemn, as if he were the possessor of knowledge quite hidden from ordinary men."[6]

When at last he begins to shamanize, he does so in a trancelike state, losing himself to his own inner excitement. The very term *Shaman* derives from a Manchurian word meaning "to excite oneself, to start up in anger, to hit out, or to dance." This state of ecstasy, which he himself commands, has been described as "a journey into the land of souls, the beyond, the underworld or the sky or over wide geographical areas—real, known regions."[7] So intense are these inner states and so poetically are they formulated by the Shaman that bystanders find themselves participating in the journey (in some instances, even when the observer is a trained anthropologist).

It is in this way that the Shaman liberates the other members of his hunting community by turning them on, each to his own personal vision. By freeing each to get with himself, the Shaman opens each hunter on to a wellspring of wonder and an inner source of power. He cannot help to heal any particular hunter without experiencing all that the other endures, experiencing it within himself with full intensity. For the Shaman the healing is a repetition or a renewal of the healing of himself through a creative act with the other. And each hunter can then transform a bit of this power to keep for himself.

Thus the Shaman of the hunting society holds office by virtue of personal spiritual attainment. According to the needs of the moment, he can deal individually with others in personal ways, improvising to meet them in the everyday world with all of its shifting perplexities. The Shaman's immediacy and improvisation can do justice, as the Priest's rituals cannot, "to everyday happenings and to the lifelong problems of man, in which an unchanging law can only dimly be discerned."[8]

In contrast, the priesthood of the planting society is often a hereditary tribal office, supernatural, all-embracing, and remote. The guidance offered by the Priest occurs at ceremonially appointed times, is general in nature, and is often of a predestined order. The Priest serves a benevolent power and is himself, by definition, good. He stands for the "moral order of things and for all that is certain in the universe."[9]

A Priest may well reflect the background of a group's philosophy of life, but the Shaman stands in the foreground. He deals in the now, as it is, bringing his own person to meet the person of each of the others whom he would guide. He turns each man toward his own inner vision.

The Eskimo Shaman Igjugarjuk tells us: "All true wisdom is only found far from men, out in the great solitude, and it can be acquired only through suffering. Privations and sufferings are the only things that can open a man's mind to that which is hidden from others."[10]

Many of the latter-day Shamans of remaining hunting and gathering societies have lost their purity of vision and become mere tricksters. "No longer the victim of cosmic oppression, [he] does not spontaneously obtain a real trance and is obliged to induce a semitrance with the help of narcotics or to mime the journey of the soul in dramatic form."[11] In this corruption of the Shaman, what once was a spontaneous losing of the self now becomes a mock shadow simulation or role playing.

5   Metaphors from Judaism

The Torah is the Hebrew name for the Pentateuch, the first five books of the Bible, the history of God's chosen people. The Talmud is the Law that tells the Jew how to apply the Torah to daily life. And so, for a man to be a talmudist and a Teacher of Torah is no small thing.

THE TEACHER OF TORAH

A parable comes down to us across the centuries, which are but a moment in God's eye. It tells us that when a teacher wishes a young boy to study the Torah, a boy too young to understand how meaningful a thing this is to do, the teacher says to him: "Read, and I shall give you nuts, and figs, and honey." And the boy makes an effort, not because of the sweetness of the reading, but because of the sweetness of the eating. As the boy grows older, no longer to be tempted by sweets, his teacher says to him: "Read, and I shall buy you fine shoes and garments." Again the boy reads, not for the fine text, but for the fine clothing. As the boy reaches young manhood, and the new clothes become less important to him, his teacher now tells him: "Learn this paragraph, and I shall give you a dinar, or perhaps even two dinars." The young man studies now to attain not the learning, but the money. And still later, as his studies continue into his adult life, when even a bit of money comes to mean less to him, his teacher will now say to him: "Learn, so that you may become an elder and a judge, that the people honor you and rise before you, as they do before this one and that." Even at this stage of life, then, this student learns, not in order to exalt the Lord, but so that he himself will be exalted by other men.

"All this is contemptible," we are told by Maimonides, a learned talmudist of the twelfth century, contemptible because "wisdom must not be pursued with a motive, not in order to obtain honors from men, not to gain money, and not to provide for oneself by the study of God's Torah."[1] A man's only purpose in learning Torah should be to know wisdom itself in order the he might live by it. A perfect man, one such as Abraham, would be able to see this clearly, and he would act accordingly.

But just here in his discourse, just at this moment of seeming righteousness, does Maimonides reveal himself as a teacher in a most human tradition. At the same time that he is honoring this selfless devotion to Torah, he also points out that it is "surpassingly difficult and not every man can grasp it, and that even if he does grasp it, he cannot affirm it at the beginning of his meditations." He sees that a man acts for the most part either to gain an advantage or to avoid harm, and that it would be hard to convince him of the sense of acting on any other basis. And so, just as with the boy of the parable whom the Teacher of Torah is helping to study, others may be offered hope of reward as an initial basis of faith. Many may thus be strengthened in their intentions, and some few may even come to learn and to do right for its own sake. Maimonides teaches that we must meet people where they are until they are strengthened sufficiently to do what they must, simply because they must.

But this was only possible during the time when the Teacher of Torah could still recognize the singularity of each of his students. Later he was to become so interested in the system of the Law and in the fence of arguments around it that his talmudism ossified into "strict legalism and arid intellectualism."[2] It was in part the danger of the emotional emptiness of the tradition-bound rationalism within which Torah study was to become entrapped that led some other men to arise as mystical ecstatics of the Kabbalah.

THE MASTER OF THE KABBALAH

The Kabbalah is an old Jewish mystical search for a way to immerse oneself in the divine stream, to find union with God. At it's highest crests, guided by those learned teachers of ecstasy, the Masters of the Kabbalah, the mission of the movement was "to unseal the soul, to untie the knots that bind it."[3] The writings to be studied instructed by implication rather than by direct assertion, and thus the Teacher left much room for amplification and interpretation by the student. He was required both to have scholarly command of the holy writings

and at the same time to be engaged in free flight of mystical speculation about their significance. This curious amalgam of tradition and
intuition made such study both "deeply conservative and intensely
revolutionary."[4]

Despite the importance of such long-studied Kabbalistic texts as
the *Zohar*, the Book of Splendor, the heart of the teaching was an
oral tradition, a personal passing on by word of mouth, a study to
be undertaken in the company of another. There are, in fact, many
allusions in the literature to those things that it would have been
unseemly to write down, to that secret wisdom which one had to
learn from personal contact with the Master.

The Master of the Kabbalah taught the techniques of meditation
and preparations for ecstasy which could lead to union with God.
A central direction of this teaching was to show the student how
to give up distracting himself by having his attention drawn to concrete
things or events such as a flower or a meeting with another person.
Instead, he was helped to meditate on highly abstract spiritual matters
by concentrating on "something capable of acquiring the highest importance, without having . . . any importance of its own."[5] The objects
chosen were the letters of the Hebrew alphabet, which of course also
serve as constituents of the name of God. This then could free a
man to move toward true mystical ecstasy.

A further development of this freeing technique of particular interest to some later psychotherapists[6] was the method of "jumping and
skipping" from one combination of letters to another. The Master
taught this as an almost free play of associations, a way of meditating
in which each jump "opens a new sphere, defined by certain formal,
not material, characteristics."[7] This widened the student's consciousness, opening it to God's logic in a way suggestive of the way
in which Freud's free association technique was intended to open
the patient's mind to the wisdom of the unconscious.

Later, Masters of the Kabbalah lost any real personal contact with
their students. They became so caught up in their increasingly elaborate methodology that they were more like distant magicians and
mysterious sorcerers than like the personal spiritual guides they had
once tried to be.

THE ZADDIK

The spiritual leader and teacher who served as rabbi to the Hasidic
community was called the Zaddik. The rich legacy of legends of Hasi-

dism speak out so beautifully for themselves that it is best we begin
with one such lovely tale:

On the eve of the Day of Atonement, when the time had come to say Kol
Nidre, all the hasidim were gathered together in the House of Prayer waiting
for the rabbi. But time passed and he did not come. Then one of the women
of the congregation said to herself: "I guess it will be quite a while before
they begin, and I was in such a hurry and my child is alone in the house.
I'll just run home and look after it to make sure it hasn't awakened. I can
be back in a few minutes." She ran home and listened at the door. Everything
was quiet. Softly she turned the knob and put her head into the room—and
there stood the rabbi holding her child in his arms. He had heard the child
crying on his way to the House of Prayer, and had played with it and sung
to it until it fell asleep.[8]

Hasidism itself was a Jewish mystical movement of the eighteenth
and nineteenth centuries, a movement which brought a charm, a vitality, and a personal relevance that touched and renewed the lives
of a despairing people. It is best understood within the historical
context in which it arose.

In 1648, a horde of Cossack troops came riding and screaming out
of the Ukraine, led by their headman, Bogdan Chmielnicki. They
came to overthrow the Polish landowners, to sack and pillage in the
name of justice. On their way, they fell upon the Jewish townspeople,
because they were the lords' stewards, because they were Jews, because they were there. The men were slaughtered, their skin stripped
from their living flesh. Infants were thrown into the air and caught
on swordspoint before the eyes of their unbelieving parents. Women
were raped, and afterwards their bellies were ripped open and live
cats were sewed inside. Fire ravaged the houses and corpses lay unburied everywhere.

During the next ten years in Poland, one hundred thousand Jews
perished in this way. Life in the surviving Jewish communities of
Eastern Europe was plagued by terror and disrupted by the overflow
of fleeing refugees. It was a time of grief and of horror, and would
have been a time of total despair as well if not for the Kabbalistic
prophecy. In the old tradition of the Kabbalah, dating to medieval
times and earlier, secret meanings were ascribed to sacred writings
so that this time was designated as "the end of days." And so the
ravaged, hope-starved Jewish people took this holocaust to be, at least,
the sign that the coming of the long-awaited Messiah was at hand.

The years that followed thus became the time of false messiahs,
opportunists, and madmen who rose up in answer and declared them-

selves Savior. The Jewish community, tormented and bewildered, desperately reaching out for an end to its pain, was readily exploited by them. Chief among the false messiahs was Sabbatai Zevi, an Oriental Jew whose rise was engineered by his ruthless apostle and manager, Nathan of Gaza. Together they spread the doctrine that now all things were permitted, laws and traditions were to be set aside, and the way to salvation was to be found through depravity. So hungry were the people to give meaning to their suffering that they remained faithful to Sabbatai Zevi even when, rather than die a martyr's death, he accepted conversion to Islam and the secular power tendered by the Sultan of Turkey. Nathan of Gaza convinced many of his followers that this, too, was a part of the salvation scheme in which evil must first reach its apogee. Large numbers of Jews then followed him to Islam, just as others would later follow the heretic and false messiah, Jacob Frank, into Christianity. European Jewry was left wracked by internal dissension and desperate for some promise that their suffering had meaning, that they had not been abandoned by God.

In their confusion and desperation, many Jews turned back to the age-old study and debating of the Jewish Law of the Talmud, hoping that this might renew their sense that they were living by something in which they could believe. But the rabbinical and talmudic way had hardened into impersonal obsession over legalisms. It had become wisdom which could fill their minds but not their hearts.

Still others looked once more to the interpreters of the Kabbalah, the guardians of esoteric truths. From these masters of hidden meanings of this complex theosophical system, they hoped to learn how to hasten the coming of the true Messiah. But it was the self-deluded Kabbalists who had led them in accepting false messiahs, and they offered to the people only secrets that the people could not understand out of their own experience.

It was then that Hasidism arose, offering a new mysticism so personal and so relevant that during the eighteenth and nineteenth centuries almost half the Jews in Eastern Europe could be numbered among its followers. In certain ways, Humanistic Psychotherapy is very much within the tradition of Hasidism. And too, there are ways in which Hasidism was both an outgrowth of, and a protest against, certain aspects of the Kabbalistic tradition. They are not unlike the ways in which the spirit of Humanistic Psychology stands over against the earlier psychoanalytic tradition, to which it is indebted and from which it has been liberated.

In order to help to bring about the coming of the Messiah and the redemption of Israel and of the world, a man must follow the law in its every injunction, practice mystical prayer, and bring certain types of mystical intention to his prayers and to his daily behavior. So the deteriorated Kabbalistic tradition told him. But at the same time, ordinary men must come to accept that what is intended in all of this is not open to their direct understanding. Like the orthodox psychoanalysts, the Kabbalists pointed out that the real meaning of things was hidden and that the way to these truths lay in the interpretation of secret symbols. The way was open only to a special few, genuine esoterics who had demonstrated the "attainment of the scholar and self-abnegation of the ascetic."[9]

These later analysts of the Kabbalah now assigned numerical values to each letter according to its place in the alphabet, added up the sum of the letters in each word, and felt free to interchange words of equal sum in order to arrive at the "true" meaning of a passage. Thus the literal meaning of the texts was frequently contradicted by their interpretations, and they felt great confidence in their fantastic speculations about the nature of God and man, and about how to overcome their estrangement. Like many later analysts, they were humorless seekers after the meanings hidden from the multitudes, taking themselves too seriously and the world too lightly. There was a total absence of dialogue with the uninitiated. Only if the ordinary layman would forego his immediate experience of himself in the world, accept a special mystical vocabulary, and transplant himself into a universe of strange symbolism, could be approach the receivers of secret learning.

In contrast to this, in the Hasidic tradition nothing is esoteric, for the meanings are no longer mysteries sealed away from the eyes of ordinary men. Rather, "everything is fundamentally open to all, and everything is reiterated again and again so simply and concretely that each man of real faith can grasp it."[10] This message, which brought the meaning of each man's life back into his own hands, was first brought to the Jews of the eighteenth century by the first Zaddik, Rabbi Israel ben Eliezer, known as the Baal Shem Tov, the master of the good name of God.

Like the Kabbalistic scholars, the Baal Shem Tov wanted to be a teacher and a helper of others, but unlike them, he would not be a high priest or wizard who initiated his flock into mysteries that they could not quite own. Neither would he be an impersonal vessel or medium through which great powers operated, nor the great scholar or seat of religious reason. Rather, as the Zaddik, he would first of all be a person in his own right, one who helped those who trusted him and was able to help only because they trusted him.

There were those who became concerned when they heard that the Baal Shem Tov had given an amulet to each of his followers and that it was said to contain within it the secret names of God. He was challenged for allegedly participating in the magic which he condemned. But when one of the amulets was opened by his critics, it was found to contain a bit of paper with only the name of the Baal Shem Tov written on it. The amulet held his name and thus represented him. It was a commitment, "nothing but a sign and pledge of the personal bond between the helper and the one who is given help, a bond based on trust."

Thus, the relationship between the Zaddik and his disciple was the crucial factor in this attempt to give spiritual help, just as the relationship between therapist and patient is crucial in its secular equivalent. The personality of the teacher takes the place of doctrine. Even this must be guarded against turning into dogma. As we read the stories of the many Zaddiks, we see that what best characterized them was their dissimilarity, their startling individuality. This was not always pleasing at first to those people who wanted not only help, but also a model, a way of behaving which they could emulate. And so in one story the followers of Rabbi Zusya asked him, "Rabbi, tell us, why do you teach in this way when Moses taught in another way?" "When I get to the coming world," answered Rabbi Zusya, "there they will not ask me, 'Why were you not more like Moses?' but instead they will ask me, 'Why were you not more like Zusya?'"

The Zaddik also values the uniqueness of each of his followers. Hasidism teaches that in each person there is something precious, and only his, that is to be found in no other person. If each man did not have a special meaning of his own, then surely God would have had no reason to put him into this world. But while each wants to be special, too often he may want to be special in the same way as another rather than in and for himself. And so in Hasidism there developed the tradition of breaking away from tradition. When a disciple had emerged as a teacher in his own right and was challenged as to why he did not follow his Zaddik's example and live as he did, he replied, "On the contrary, I do follow his example, for I leave him, as he left his teacher."

The Zaddik, unlike the later Kabbalist or the psychoanalyst, did not remain a mysterious figure, detached from those he helped, offering only symbolic interpretations of what is hidden. Instead, he shared himself with the person who came for help. He did not necessarily reveal himself directly, but he came through as a person in the very ways in which he concealed himself as a teacher. He answered questions on a level other than that on which they were asked, often by telling stories or sharing experiences of his own. These tales had a basic human feeling that instructed despite the apparent absence of intellectual content. They stirred the hearer partly because of their primitive spiritual character and the ways in which they caught at his own secret needs. But most important they provided a way in which the Zaddik offered a part of himself, an expression of the possibility of fundamental strength and tenderness of the relationship.

The Zaddik was a helper who would extend his hand to a follower, and if the follower would take it, he would guide him until he was able to find his way alone. Yet, he must never relieve the one he is helping of the responsibility of doing for himself whatever he has grown strong enough to do. At no time might he free anyone of the burden of what he must do for himself. No one can take the place of another. And as Rabbi Baer points out: "What you don't get by your own work, you don't have."

At the same time, the Zaddik had to participate in a way that risked his own deep personal involvement. He must be willing to be close to another and to get caught up in his troubles. The Baal Shem Tov tells us: "If you want to raise a man from mud and filth, do not think it is enough to keep standing on top and reaching down to him a helping hand. You must go all the way down yourself, down into the mud and filth. You must not hesitate to get yourself dirty."

In a curious way, what the Zaddik had to offer was himself. If someone could really learn to be with him, he would have learned what he needed to know. The Zaddik was not merely the apostle of Hasidic teaching, but the bearer of it. He did not teach Torah, he became Torah. He *was* the teaching. He was its working reality for the disciple. It was his life and his personal freedom rather than his knowledge which had religious value for his followers. As one student said of his Zaddik, "I did not go to the Maggid of Meritz to learn Torah from him but to watch him tie his bootlaces."

Sometimes the Zaddik was caught between what he felt he must do on the one hand and what he thought he ought to do on the other. Rabbi Bunam told of a time when he felt the need to tell a certain story, but was tempted not to because it was so worldly and would surely arouse vulgar laughter. He feared that his followers would respond by no longer considering him a rabbi. Nonetheless, he decided to follow his inner feelings and told the story. The result, he said, was that "the gathering burst out laughing. And those who up to this point had been distant from me attached themselves to me." Thus, it was the Zaddik's act of risking simply being himself through trusting his feelings and acting on them that engaged a like commitment from his followers.

So too with the psychotherapist, the significant part of what is therapeutic is not just the knowledge, strategies, or reinforcement schedules that he brings to the hour but the way in which he can be with the patient. When the therapist is himself and acts on what he feels, he is therapeutic. This is less a matter of his simple confidence in his own feelings than it is willingness to surrender to the compelling qualities of his experience of the patient. Thus it is told that when a famous Zaddik who did not conceive of himself as a healer was confronted with a sick child, "without any faith in his own gift, in the urgent need of the moment, Rabbi Yisakhar took the child in his arms, laid it in the cradle, rocked it, prayed, and succeeded in healing it."

Admittedly, it is more difficult for the young rabbi or the novice therapist to trust his feelings, and so for a while he must be guided more by rules and expectations. At first he may be tempted to take his powers too seriously, as did young Rabbi Mendel when he boasted to his teacher that in the mornings and the evenings he saw the angels who rolled back the darkness and the light. "Yes," answered his teacher, "in my youth I saw that, too. Later on you don't see those things any more." Or the beginner may overestimate how far he has come without seeing how far he has yet to go. So it was with the disciples of Rabbi Pinhas when he found them seated in the House of Study gravely discussing how afraid they were that the Evil Urge would pursue them. "Don't worry," he assured them; "you have not gotten high enough for it to pursue you. For the time being, you are still pursuing it." Of course, it is difficult to learn to take oneself seriously enough without taking oneself too seriously. As the saying goes, a man must have two pockets into which he can reach at one time or another according to his needs. In his right pocket he must keep the words: "For my sake was the world created." And in his left: "I am dust and ashes."

Eventually, as the young rabbis achieve greater spiritual growth, they develop new ways of serving God, each according to his own character. As each becomes more his own particular sort of teacher, he increases his capacity and willingness to give himself over to the situation with the other by bringing more of himself to it. In so doing, he points to the Hasidic understanding of the problems which occur between people;[11] that is, that in dealing with the conflicts which arise between man and man, each man must begin with himself. A man is not merely an object to be examined, with problems to be analyzed away, but a person who is called upon to "straighten himself out." Rather than simply blaming the other person with whom he is struggling, he must take on the difficult responsibility of turning his attention to his own part in this, with no more than the hope that the other will do the same for himself. One way of stating this task in Hasidic terms would be: the origin of the conflicts which I experience between myself and others is to be found in the fact that too often *I do not know what I feel, I do not say what I mean,* and *I do not do what I say.* It is in large part a matter of being honest with myself. Everything depends on myself, and only I can straighten myself out.

The Zaddik and the therapist, each in his own terms, can point the way by venturing his own honest facing up, by exposing his own heart-searching. He must show that this is a part of the human struggle that is never solved once and for all by anyone, no matter how holy or how mature he may be. Thus when the Baal Shem Tov was asked how one could tell whether or not a teacher is a real Zaddik, he suggested that the teacher be asked for advice on how to rid oneself permanently of temptation to evil, how to expel alien thoughts forever. If he can give such advice, then he is of no real importance as a teacher. For with the Evil Urge, "a man must struggle until his last moment, and just that is the service of a man in the world."

What is more, even the urge to evil is a kind of vitality, a life source to be reclaimed rather than rejected. We need to be in touch with and hopefully to own every part of ourselves so that we do not continue to be ar war within ourselves. If a thief comes in the night, and we cry out and so scare him off, nothing is accomplished beyond the moment, and we must remain in fear. But if we do not alarm the thief, but let him draw near enough so that we may lay hold of him and bind him, then we have the chance of reforming him. So, too, our own willful impulses can become a rich source of renewal of imaginative powers. Our stubbornness can be transformed into determination, and our struggle with the other can surrender into intimacy. Each man must confront himself in order to accomplish these transformations, this turning of the self.

This *turning* stands at the very heart of the Jewish conception of a man's way in the world. Each man must face up not only ritually on the Day of Atonement, but at each moment. Each present moment is a moment of redemption. And as Rabbi David of Lelov tells us, a man can only be redeemed to the extent to which he recognizes himself. He must stand up squarely to himself, confront his troubles, and turn himself toward setting himself to rights. In this way, each man is capable of renewing himself from within and of recommitting himself anew to taking his place with other men in God's world. What is the proper time for this turning? *If not now, when?*

But then, how is a man to retain this commitment to turning, in the face of daily frustrations and frequent disappointments, betrayal by people whom he trusts, and the loss of people whom he loves? At times a man needs counsel and aid, a hand extended to him. But how is the helper to be of help in such matters? It is said that the Baal Shem Tov is best remembered not for his miraculous deeds, but for the fact that on the Sabbath his heart beat so loudly in his fear of God that all could hear it. It was knowing him as a person in the depths of his feelings which offered hope to the Hasidic followers. Of course, he was also the possessor of wisdom, but of what kind? To answer this, Rabbi Hayyim described the skills with which he led his congregation. He likened his followers to men lost in a great forest. They chanced upon another man who had been lost even longer. Not realizing this, they asked him to lead them out of the woods. His reply was, "That I cannot do. But I can point out the ways that lead further into the thicket, and after that let us try to find the way together."

In part, what the Zaddik must do to help was to interest the man in the potential struggle within each of us. However, this struggle within oneself must not be confused with some self-sorry brooding over those things in the world that one cannot change by any act of will. For I may "rake the muck this way, rake the muck that way—it will always be muck. In the time I am brooding over it, I could be stringing pearls for the delight of Heaven."[12] The searching of the heart must involve a genuine willingness to face up to our losses, to bury our dead, and to mourn their passing as we helplessly give them up. Otherwise, there is only a sterile self-torture, a stubborn holding on which leads to the despair of not living with things as they are. What we have been through we cannot change, and what approaches we cannot know beforehand. We must accept that "the moment is God's moment; therefore, we can, indeed, prepare ourselves ever again for the deed, but we cannot prepare the deed itself."[13]

This commitment to things as they are must be understood, in part, in terms of the Baal Shem Tov's reinterpretation of the late-Kabbalistic creation myth of the Divine Sparks. In one version, the trouble began in a primordial time when worlds were still being built and torn down again by God. In another, the fall of Adam, whose soul contained all souls, marked the time when the sparks of God's divine creativity were scattered throughout the world. In either case, the sparks were said to have permeated all matter, with the result that some of God's divinity was trapped and so is estranged from Him, and man along with it. It is man's task in the world to free the sparks from imprisonment and thus to restore them to God, thereby bringing about salvation. The Kabbalists said that this must come about by secret ritual means. The false messiahs said it must occur by a descent into evil. But Hasidism tells us that to recover the divine sparks, which are everywhere, we must *hallow everyday life.*

If the sparks are present in every material shell, in every plant and animal and man, then there is no longer a distinction between the sacred and the profane. All has become holy. And so the Baal Shem Tov taught: "Joy in the world as it is, in life as it is, in every hour of life in this world, as that hour is."

No set action was any longer central. It was the dedication of all of one's actions which now became decisive. The Zaddik did not teach *what* to do, but instead, through the relationship, he communicated *how* to do things. He taught that the way to live is with all of your being; that whatever you have to do at one time or another, you must give yourself to it. Someone asked the disciple of a great Zaddik, "What are the most important things in life for your teacher?" "Always just what he is engaged in at the moment," replied the disciple.

The religious fervor which, before Hasidism, had been directed to the future, to the coming of the Messiah, was now given to God and to man in the world at each present moment. Relationship with other men in the world was now seen as the closest approach to being with God. Thus, Hasidism does not recognize any distinction between religion and ethics. Devotion has become the responsibility each of us has for his own life, for the bit of the world entrusted to his care.

This commitment to life among other men does not negate a man's need to be by, with, and for himself as well. As Rabbi Moshe Leib has said: "A human being who has not a single hour for his own every day is no human being." At times, it is first necessary for a man to descend into the depths of his own solitary being if he is then to be able to experience the world in which he wanders in all of its dimensions. Solitude provides the substance which is then realized in communion, as the Baal Shem Tov told us when he admonished: "Learn to keep silent, in order that you may know how to speak."

Though solitude and communion are both necessary and do in part serve to renew the depth of one another, a man must decide for himself at which point to give up one for the other. When the questions are posed as to why we have curtains if we want people to look in, and why we have a window at all if we do not want them to look in, Rabbi Eleazar answers simply, "When you want someone you love to look in, you draw aside the curtain."

Furthermore, even to be with others does not imply a life of selfless service. When Rabbi Elimelekh found that one of the guests at his table had not begun to eat with the others, he asked the man why this was so. His guest humbly replied, "I have no spoon." "Look," said the Zaddik, "one must know enough to ask for a spoon, and a plate, too, if need be!" And if others offend, a man must be prepared to deal with this too—not with wildly destructive rage, but with a kind of tamed anger which he keeps in his pocket. When he needs it, he must be sure to take it out.

Hasidism has a great reverence for life and an openness toward the world. It teaches not only a spiritual lustiness and a warm feeling for the moment at hand, but also a joy in the sensual life, a joy which hallows and sanctifies that life. Salvation is not a reward for self-sacrifice and ascetic denial of the body, but the ecstasy of giving oneself to life. Rabbi Israel of Rizhyn believed that God created man as he is, not "to be caged in his lusts, but to be free in them." It is the calling of the Zaddik and of the psychotherapist to help men to free themselves. When a Hasid gives himself over to the ecstasy of singing, of dancing, of making love, each of these becomes a way of praying.

As is the case with all of man's best efforts, Hasidism eventually fell into a state of corruption. The Hasid's fervent love of the Zaddik declined into reverence for a great magician. The place of the spiritual teacher was elevated into a special relation with God, from which he could use his exaggerated powers to intercede for his followers without their having to strain to accomplish for themselves. The very position of Zaddik became a power-laden gift to be bestowed by dynastic succession. Communities led by different Zaddiks vied for position as followers of the most miraculous teacher, slandering the leaders of other communities in fierce competition. They had forgotten that God made a place for everyone in the world and that people only feel crowded if they wish to occupy the place of another.

This tragic degradation of Hasidism could not have occurred if the Zaddiks themselves had not been tempted into the arrogance of mis-using their gifts and offices in the service of petty triumphs. They threw off the "holy insecurity," the need to live without certainty and yet with faith and humor, and so courted the debasing of their calling. If we consider this aspect of the history of Hasidism, perhaps we may derive yet one more bit of instruction from that lovely mystical movement, though this time in the form of a sad object lesson.

6 *Metaphors from Christianity*

THE CURER OF SOULS

Jesus is the Lamb of God, and Jesus is the Shepherd of His Flock. The traditional role for the pastor as the Curer of Souls is as old as Christianity itself. It began in the ministry of Jesus, was formalized within the Roman Catholic Church, and has endured as a significant function of contemporary Protestant clergy. Pastoral care is a special and many-sided ministry, which "consists of helping acts, done by representative Christian persons, directed toward the healing, sustaining, guiding, and reconciling of troubled persons whose troubles arise in the context of ultimate meanings and concerns."[1] In this definition, "representative Christian person" does not necessarily imply that the helper be a clergyman. He may instead be a layman who professes the faith and brings it to bear upon the suffering of another person, for the sake of that particular person.

The matter of the troubles' being those that "arise in the context of ultimate meaning and concern" can be misleading. For example, once in a clinical training program for clergymen at a state mental hospital, there was one young minister who was self-serious to the point of being grave. He wanted to be sure to have an opportunity to work with a patient whose problems were truly religious, clearly matters of ultimate concern. A patient was selected to whom the minister was to offer pastoral care. The patient was a profoundly depressed man in his thirties who felt a deep sense of unexplained guilt. He complained of the absence of any central meaning to his life and was obsessed with searching for the answer to the question, "Who am I?"

The young minister was righteously dissatisfied with being saddled with this patient who was "just depressed," rather than having someone assigned who had truly religious problems. His supervisor solved the problem. Apologetically, he withdrew the first patient and substituted a second. The new choice was a woman in menopause who had a single, and this time an undeniably religious, preoccupation. The central experience of her life, and practically the only thing about which she would talk to anyone, was what was happening to her every night. Each time the lights were put out on her ward and things quieted down, the Lord God would come to her very own bed, slip in under the covers, and have intercourse with her.

To his credit, the young minister talked his feelings out with his supervisor. He was helped by the pastoral care he himself received and opted for working with the first patient to whom he had originally been assigned. Ultimate meaning and concern can be revealed in unexpected ways.

Let us now look more carefully at the four functions of pastoral care, at what the Curer of Souls is actually about: the healing, sustaining, guiding, and reconciling. Although one or another of these functions has come to the fore at different points in the history of Christianity, they are interrelated, as well as each being important in its own right.

When the Curer of Souls heals, he does not merely restore the health of the troubled person. Rather, his healing has the quality of making the person "whole," thus leaving him in better condition than before he developed the trouble which was to be healed. For example, a person's illness can create a spiritual crisis in his life, particularly if he is seriously incapacitated or faces death. Christian healing, at that point, could well include the spiritual reintegration that can come with a man's reevaluating the priorities in his life. In this way, he may end up being spiritually "healthier" after the healing than he had been before the onset of the illness.

Traditionally, one of the ways in which this healing could be achieved was by anointing the body of the troubled person with oil which had been blessed. The troubles or bad feelings were earlier experienced metaphorically as unclean spirits or demons. Consequently, the oil was usually placed on the bodily orifices. Through what other portals could the demons have entered?

A second means of carrying out this healing ministry of the Christian church is by bringing the sick person into contact with holy relics. Typically, these relics are bits and pieces thought to be parts of the remains of the bodies of saints or of artifacts associated with the life of Jesus (such as a piece of the cross on which He was crucified). This residual healing power was sometimes institutionalized by the erection of shrines to which the troubled could come to be healed. Unfortunately, it also allowed unscrupulous hustlers to pawn off enough remains of the cross to have built a church with.

Still another form which the Christian healing ministry takes is the laying on of hands. Here the victim of the affliction is touched by a charismatic person who has special healing powers. So it was with Jesus:

> And there came a leper to him, beseeching him, and kneeling down to him, and saying unto him, If thou wilt, thou canst make me clean.
> And Jesus moved with compassion, put forth *his* hand, and touched him, and saith unto him, I will: be thou clean.
> And as soon as he had spoken, immediately the leprosy departed from him, and he was cleansed.[2]

And, finally, malevolent spirits or demons can be driven away by means of special rituals and incantations or by making them leave one body to enter another. So it was with a certain madman, a man who had unclean spirit and lived among the tombs. This man cried out to Jesus:

> . . . What have I to do with thee, Jesus, thou Son of the most high God? I adjure thee by God, that thou torment me not.
> For he said unto him, Come out of the man, *thou* unclean spirit.
> And he asked him, What is thy name? And he answered, saying, My name is Legion: for we are many.
> And he besought him much that he would not send them away out of the country.
> Now there was there nigh unto the mountains a great herd of swine feeding.
> And all the devils besought him, saying, Send us into the swine, that we may enter into them.
> And forthwith Jesus gave them leave. And the unclean spirits went out, and entered into the swine: and the herd ran violently down a steep place into the sea, (they were about two thousand:) and were choked in the sea.[3]

Later when people came to see what had happened, they found the madman seated at the feet of Jesus. He was at peace, free of demons at last and in his right mind. This method of healing is called exorcism. As in the case of many other aspects of pastoral care, equivalent functions can be found in non-Christian religions as well.

Another aspect of the work of the Curer of Souls is *sustaining*. It is perhaps more complex and less concrete than healing, but it is at least as significant. It is a task which involves, first, preserving the troubled person's situation with a minimum of loss. Next, it is important to help the victim to see that whatever his losses may be, he has one consolation: no loss negates his possibilities in relationship with God. Then, too, it is necessary to help the victim to consolidate whatever resources remain to him. And, finally, redemption is possible. If the loss is really accepted, it can help the person to go on to have what he might from the rest of his life. Thus, in the role of sustainer, the Curer of Souls helps the troubled person to accept his losses, to face things as they are, and to go on.

Still another important function of pastoral care is *guidance*. This involves helping a troubled person through the crisis of making difficult decisions. This guidance is based on the wisdom of Christianity and ranges from sympathetic listening to the giving of direct advice. During the Middle Ages, the ministry of guidance was largely involved in devil-craft, that is, in helping a man so that he need not stand alone against Satan. Later, the metaphors. of conflict changed, but the recognition of the importance of decision making and of commitment continued.

Rounding out the functions of pastoral care is *reconciliation*. In the hands of the Curer of Souls, this means helping to establish or to renew relationships between alienated people and their neighbors as well as between such people and God. This can be accomplished by inspiring a feeling of forgiveness in the troubled person. At times, the reconciliation is attempted by discipline, that is, by admonishing people to be good. However, it is more likely to be effective when the Curer of Souls can put people in touch with the essential humanness of us all and with God's love for each man. And so it was with Jesus:

And the scribes and Pharisees brought unto him a woman taken in adultery; and when they had set her in the midst,

They say unto him, Master, this woman was taken in adultery, in the very act.

Now Moses in the law commanded us, that such should be stoned: but what sayest thou?

. . . So when they continued asking him, he lifted himself up, and said unto them, He that is without sin among you, let him first cast a stone at her.

. . . And they which heard it, being convicted by their own conscience, went out one by one, beginning at the eldest, even unto the last: and Jesus was left alone, and the woman standing in the midst.

When Jesus had lifted up himself, and saw none but the woman, he said unto her, Woman, where are those thine accusers? hath no man condemned thee?

She said, No man, Lord. And Jesus said unto her, Neither do I condemn thee: go, and sin no more.[4]

Each of these functions of pastoral care is subject to abuse by righteous, manipulative people who still take on the role of Curer of Souls.

It is very tempting to decide what is best for others, to confuse our own secret needs with what is "for their own good."

THE CONFESSOR

One gets the impression that men have always had the need to share their secrets with others, especially those secrets about which they felt guilty. In the sharing they have sought respite from their loneliness, reassurance as to their worth, and expiation of their guilt. In the Christian Church, this inclination of man has been raised to the level of duty, ritualized in its conduct, and given a formal agent for its mediation, the Confessor.

The curious history of Christian confession begins with scriptural foundation in Jesus' bestowing on His Apostles the authority to deal with the sins of men: "And I will give unto thee the keys of the kingdom of heaven: and whatsoever thou shalt bind on earth shall be bound in heaven: and whatsoever thou shalt loose on earth shall be loosed in heaven";[5] and more specifically, "Whose soever sins ye remit, they are remitted unto them; *and* whose soever *sins* ye retain, they are retained."[6]

In order for those so empowered to be able to judge each case, they must hear out the confession of the penitent. This need to know the particulars of each sin was, in fact, spelled out in Church law by the council of Trent. During the first four hundred years after the coming of Christ, personal confession in the early Christian Church was made in public. People lived in small communities in which their sins were often directed against their neighbors. It seems fitting, then, that it was before these offended members of their community that men confessed and did penance. In another sense, the confession itself (rather than the penance) mediated the reconciliation.[7]

During the fifth century A.D., things began to change. Perhaps it was due to the reluctance of some of the more powerful or influential members of these communities. It is not certain, but it was at this time that the church began to "seal" confession.[8] What this amounted to was that increasingly the confession, the sin, and the ensuing penitence, all of which had once been public, now became a private matter between sinner and Confessor. Seven hundred years later, this trend had been finalized as an absolute and universal practice in the Church.

All confession was secret, and Confessors were bound not to reveal the confidences they had heard. This privacy, of course, made possible the abuses to which Martin Luther later addressed himself. Focus shifted from confession and reconciliation to penance and absolution. Confessors could sell indulgences to the rich who confessed sins, protected as they were from public scrutiny. The Reformation, of course, eliminated the one remaining human intermediary, leaving each man a priest, directly accountable to God. Nonetheless, to this day, Protestant parishioners come to their clergymen to confess and to seek the help offered by pastoral counselors.

In addition to the corruption of the role of the Confessor to which Martin Luther objected, there has developed a curious corruption in the person who is confessing. In the Roman Catholic Church, the sinner confesses to the Confessor, is heard out, judged, and given penance to do. If he does the penance, is sincerely repentant, and intends to avoid further occasions of sin, he is given God's forgiveness, mediated by the Confessor. But some sinners reject God's forgiveness: they know better than God. They are still guilty and do not forgive themselves. This is a sin of pride known as scrupulosity.[9]

Another problem is, of course, the weakness of the vessel—the Confessor. I shall not wrestle here with the theological problems of the relation between the Confessor, the man, and the Confessor, the intermediary of God. However, there is a very revealing short story by F. Scott Fitzgerald entitled "Absolution,"[10] which deals with the confessional. In this story, the Confessor is a young priest "with cold watery eyes, who, in the still of the night, wept cold tears." His problem is revealed when one warm afternoon he is unable to do the Lord's work by concentrating on the confession of an eleven-year-old boy who sits uncomfortably before the priest in his study.

The boy is frightened because he has sinned. He has done terrible things. He has told his father a lie. He has taken the Lord's name in vain. He has been mean to an old lady. He has smoked in the barn. The priest, his Confessor, has great difficulty in giving himself over to be God's intermediary, in judging and forgiving the sins of this boy. Mainly, it is difficult for the young priest because he is again and again distracted by the "rustle of Swede girls along the path by his window." Their laughter and their soft voices make him think of the night when "all along the land there would be these blonde Northern girls and the tall young men from the farms lying out beside the wheat, under the moon."

THE SPIRITUAL FATHER IN THE DESERT

Four centuries after Christ had walked the land, certain holy men went on long spiritual pilgrimages. They went to live as hermits in the deserts of Egypt, Palestine, and Syria. Antony was the first, and other men flocked after him for a hundred years. The names of some of these men are remembered to this day, names such as Antony himself, Basil, and Jerome. Most of the names have long been forgotten. Yet the impact of the spiritual tradition of these Desert Fathers lives on.

These abbots often went to live out their lives in desert caves. They committed their gaze to eternity, their habits to austerity, and their persons to solitude. Paradoxically, their ways taught other men much more about their own everyday lives than about eternity. The consciousness of later generations has been affected by the ways in which the Desert Fathers denied the final importance of life on earth. They taught men who came after them to evaluate their experiences more clearly by quality than by duration. Instead of discrediting time by setting it over against eternity, they refocused men on the depth of meaning which each moment can bring. They taught men how to make themselves eternal, hour by hour, in this world.

The Desert Fathers not only sought their own salvation but also offered instruction and spiritual advice to others. Young monks and disciples would come to the Desert Fathers for guidance. Traditionally, they would state their problem, perhaps in the form of some temptation with which they struggled. The young man would then entreat the Desert Father saying, "Speak to me a word of salvation." The answers given were most often simple, direct, and personal.

The Desert Fathers did not rely on admonishment. Their primary way of teaching was by example, and only later by their words. So it was when a brother came to Abba Poemen and said:

"Some brothers are living with me; do you wish me to command them?"
The old man replied: "Not at all. Act first, and if they wish to 'live' they will put the lesson into effect themselves."
The brother said: "Abba, they themselves want me to command them."
The old man said: "No, become a model for them, and not a lawgiver."[11]

Sometimes the Desert Father must be hard on the young disciple. Young brothers had especially difficult times with the solitude of this life. They came to the Desert Father not for guidance but to be rescued. So it was with a certain young brother who sought a word from Abba Moses in Scete. The old man said to him, "Go and sit in thy cell, and thy cell shall teach thee all things."[12] But if his sayings were sometimes hard, this was to help the young man to do what he must, no matter how disconcerting. Abba Moses' advice, for example, was a way of turning the young brother toward the naked reality of his own solitude. It is crucial that the hard sayings not arise from a secret need to dominate on the part of the teacher.

Despite the isolation of living in solitary cells, the matter of the young monk's being able to have direct contact with a living teacher was crucial. Antony says, "The monk must make known to the elders every step he takes and every drop of water he drinks in his cell to see if he is not doing it wrong."[13]

There is, of course, an irony to a solitude that must be revealed to others. This irony pervades the tradition of the Spiritual Fathers in the Desert. The monk seeks out the solitude of the desert as the condition for salvation, being "alone to the alone."[14] It is a way of seeking a confrontation with God, one to One. And yet, it is at just such a time that "the giant agony of the world" cannot long be ignored.[15] And, indeed, it is Antony, the first of these hermits, who said, "With our neighbor is life and death."[16]

The meaning of the solitude must be examined and re-examined. It is quite possible to be in one's cell for the wrong reasons. In the end it may turn out that solitude and other apparently virtuous seekings are no more than subtle ways of stubbornly and pridefully showing off the self to the self. At its best, life alone in a cell is a way of accepting loneliness. The help of others can be useful, but first a man must help himself. In the solitude of the cell, the young monk must wrestle with his demons, face his illusions, and resist his temptations. And so it is that life in the cell has been described as "being in a fiery furnace," and "when you do not live worthily in your cell, the cell of its own accord, vomits you out."[17]

An important part of the Desert Father's spiritual guidance is his way of directing the young monk back to his cell, turning him back to dealing with himself. But this instruction is to no avail unless the brother is helped to understand that he must return to the giving-in to solitude. If he merely returns to his cell to give himself over to bitterness and hostile fantasies about other men, he might as well not return to his cell at all. As Abba Lucius tells us, "Unless thou first amend thy life going to and fro amongst men, thou shalt not avail to amend it dwelling alone."[18] Some men are not yet ready to benefit from the solitude of the cell.

Some young monks were perturbed by how little they felt they could use the solitude. To such a one as this, a Desert Father said, "Sit thou in thy cell, and do what thou canst, and be not troubled; for the little that thou dost is even as when Antony did great things and many in the desert."[19] And there were yet other young men for whom solitude was not at all to be the path to salvation. To such a one, a vision did appear, in his cell, asking:

"Why are you so desolate and brokenhearted?"

"Because I seek the will of God."

"It is the will of God that you serve the human race, in order to reconcile it with him."

"I ask about the will of God and you tell me to serve men?"

The . . . [vision] repeats three times: "It is God's will that you serve men in order to bring them to him."[20]

There are, then, many paths to salvation, and despite their commitment to solitude the Desert Fathers understood and taught this. When Abba Nistero was asked what good work a particular man should do, the old man said, "What . . . thou findest that thy soul desireth in following God, that do, and keep thy heart."[21]

Yet in a way it is a subtler matter than it appears to be. The seeking of salvation is more a state of mind and spirit than it is the physical setting in which it is sought. And so it was also said, "It is better to have many about thee, and to live the solitary life in thy will, than to be alone, and the desire of thy mind be with the crowd."[22]

Even though the sayings of the Desert Fathers are to have some general meaning for all men, should they find themselves in similar circumstances, each was first an answer to a particular man's particular question. It was directed to helping *him,* then and there, but not in an authoritarian manner. Rather, the saying was an attempt to help the young monk to discover the nature of the will of God, for him in particular, in that time and place.

At times it was difficult for the young monks to understand why the Desert Fathers would give answers that seemed contradictory when the same question was asked by different brothers. For example:

Once Abba Joseph was reproached with this. When asked how to deal with tempting thoughts, he told one monk to resist them forcefully and thrust them out, and another to pay no attention to them. . . . The second complained of the contradiction. [He answered this more experienced questioner by saying]: " . . . I spoke to you as I would have spoken to myself."[23]

Tranquility and sweet repose must be sought by different men in differing ways.

The principles that mattered to the Desert Fathers and the ways in which they taught them become clearer as we examine their concern with austerity. It is thought that because these men lived alone, suffering the hardships of the desert and of their own self-sacrifice, that simple asceticism was uppermost for them. But this turns out not to be so.

It was Antony who pointed out that a man could wear out his body with abstinence, and yet if he lacked discretion, he would still remain a long way from God. The same obtains for a man who has given in to temptation and then seeks penance so that he will be forgiven. When asked by a monk who had committed a great sin whether he should do penance for three years or one year or for forty days, the Desert Father merely told him that each amount was quite a good deal of time. Finally, he added that he felt that three days would satisfy God, if the monk repented with his whole heart.

What is more, the Desert Fathers were wise enough not to be impressed with simple self-elevating sacrifice. And so it was that in comparing the services of two young monks, an old man said, "If that brother who carries his fast for six days were to hang himself up by the nostrils, he could not equal the other, who does service to the sick."[24]

Self-conscious austerity is no austerity at all. And so it was that when a certain monk met some nuns on the road, he fled at the sight of them. Wisely, the Abbess said to him, "Hadst thou been a perfect monk thou wouldst not have looked so close as to perceive that we were women."[25]

The Desert Fathers understood that austerity was not an end in itself. It is easy to be tempted to pride in one's humility, and so they had to learn ways to deal with this in themselves as in their disciples. And so it was that certain old men said: "If thou seest a young man ascending by his own will up to heaven catch him by the foot and throw him down upon the earth, for it is not expedient for him."[26] This was carried out in no uncertain terms:

A certain brother, having renounced the world and taken the habit, straightway shut himself up, saying, "I am minded to be a solitary." But when the older men of the neighborhood heard it, they came and threw him out and made him go round the cells of the brethren and do penance before each, saying, "Forgive me, for I am no solitary, but have only now attempted to begin to be a monk."[27]

Taken by itself, this manner of correction is somewhat misleading. When needed, the Desert Fathers could be hard, but they could also be most tender, understanding, and giving. So it was that when a young brother came to complain of how he was troubled by lustful thoughts, he was comforted. The old man encouraged him to deal with his troubled thoughts by revealing them rather than keeping them secret. And so, he came to the old man again and again and again. After eleven trips to the old man's cell, the younger man was told: "Believe me, my son, if God permitted the thoughts with which my own mind is stung to be transferred to thee, thou wouldst not endure them, but wouldst dash thyself headlong."[28]

Abba Pastor understood how hard it was for a man to face up sometimes and how he might need encouragement. Therefore, he said: "If a man has sinned and denies it not, but says 'I have sinned,' scold him not, for thou wilt break the purpose of his heart. But rather say to him, 'Be not sad, my brother, but watch thyself hereafter,' and thou wilt rouse his heart to repentance."[29]

Somewhere along the line, the tender and giving aspects of this tradition disappeared. Solitude and austerity became sources of self-torture, with each man trying to outdo the other in giving himself over to pain in this world for the sake of pleasure in the next. The Desert Fathers succumbed to their own temptations to arrogance by becoming more and more arbitrary and domineering. Their commands grew increasingly unreasonable as they moved toward cruelly insulting the dignity of the men whose spiritual guidance they were supposed to provide. Originally, the Desert Fathers had stressed asceticism as a way to overcome petty self-concern. Later it was "as if the sole purpose of ascetic training were to break down . . . personal integrity by . . . [means of] blind obedience."[30]

THE FRIEND OF GOD

The Reformation, that revolutionary sixteenth-century religious movement, which resulted in the establishment of Protestantism, was a complex sociopolitical and even economic phenomenon. The central ecclesiastical thrust of the Reformation emerged in Martin Luther's protests against Church practices, but even these religious views were fed by many streams. One important source of inspiration for Luther was Johannes Eckhart, the best known of the fourteenth-century German mystics. This pious Dominican, called Meister (Master) Eckhart, this Friend of God, had to defend himself against charges of wild mystical heresy two hundred years before the Reformation, which owed its origins to struggles such as his.

It was not that Meister Eckhart hoped to turn men against the Church—only that he hoped to turn them toward God. In the spiritual guidance which he offered, he admitted he might be guilty of error but not of heresy, "for the first has to do with mind and the second with will."[31] He was ever a yea-sayer, more for than against. He believed in trying to overwhelm lies and evil by disclosing the true and the good, rather than by fighting back with criticism and condemnation. For this Friend of God, the Divine Being was pure affirmation, to be reached not by struggle but by faith alone.

He believed that God is Love and that personal salvation, the center of life, can only be sought by direct union with God. It is this mystical merging of the knower and the known of which Meister Eckhart speaks when he tells us: "The eye with which I see God is the same as that with which he sees me."[32] He anticipates later emphasis on justification by faith rather than by works when he points out that this union cannot be achieved through external acts of penance such as fasting or going barefoot. He tells the sinner instead "to face about toward our beloved God, with unwavering affection. . . . However you accomplish this is the way for you."[33]

Even the inclination to sin, he says, is always beneficial. It is a matter of *will*, whether toward virtue or toward vice. The Kingdom of God is truly at hand within each of us, and all men can come to know this. Meditation, prayer, and opening oneself to God is all that is needed, without the intermediary of priest or sacrament. Grace and divine goodness need not be begged for but can be taken without asking.

Each man must do this in his own way, by being himself in his own life. So it was that when a priest once said to this Friend of God that he wished that he had Meister Eckhart's soul in his body instead of his own, this Christian guru replied: "You would really be foolish. That would get you nowhere—it would accomplish as little as for your soul to be in my body. No soul can really do anything except through the body to which it is attached."[34]

What is needed is that each man empty himself of things so as to fill himself with God. He is to live his life but not to desire anything more than happiness with God, for when a man lives in love and purity, "God plays and laughs."[35] Only a loving Friend of God could offer so startling a theology as that: "When God laughs at the soul and the soul laughs back at God, the persons of the trinity are begotten."[36]

This medieval Christian guru, in his sermons and in his inspiring "talks of instruction," went far beyond the gravely systematic teachings of his time. He offered to reopen the immediacy of spiritual experience to all believers. A lovely legend expresses the way of being with God in the world with which he inspired generations of German mystics who followed in his path:

Meister Eckhart met a beautiful naked boy.
He asked him where he came from.
He said: "I come from God."
Where did you leave him?
"In virtuous hearts."
Where do you find him?
"Where I part with all creatures."
Who are you?
"A king."
Where is your kingdom.
"In my heart."
Take care that no one divide it with you!
"I shall."
Then he led him to his cell.
Take whichever coat you will.
"Then I should be no king!"
And he disappeared.
For it was God himself—
Who was having a bit of fun.[37]

The teachings of Meister Eckhart took root and blossomed, only to wither away into the lifeless, hollow remnants of modern Protestantism, retaining shape without vitality. Justification by faith has too often led to good intentions without social responsibility, to more loving talk than loving action. Popularizing has encouraged a destructive reduction of moral constructs to surface "niceness," and the vagueness of mysticism has resulted in an insidious elitism of those who have attained salvation.

7 *Metaphors from the Orient*

THE COMPASSIONATE BUDDHA

A tale is told of the Buddha,[1] the Exalted One, the Possessor of the
Ten Forces, and of how he taught his doctrines to the woman Kisa
Gotami in the time of her overwhelming sorrow. Kisa Gotami, called
the Frail One, had a young son who was the sunshine of her day.
It came to pass that hardly had he grown big enough to run and
play, when he died. So great was the sorrow of Kisa Gotami that
she would not accept the boy's death.

Instead she took to the streets, carrying her dead son on her hip.
She went from house to house, knocking at each door and demanding:
"Give me medicine for my son." People saw that she was mad. They
made fun of her and told her: "There is no medicine for the dead."
But she acted as if she did not understand, and only went on asking.

Now a certain wise old man saw Kisa Gotami and understood that
it was her sorrow for her dead son that had driven her out of her
mind. He did not mock her, but instead told her: "Woman, the only
one who might know of medicine for your son is the Possessor of
the Ten Forces, he who is foremost among men and gods. Go then
to the monastery. Go then to him, and ask him about medicine for
your son."

Seeing that the wise man spoke the truth, she went with her son
on her hip to the monastery in which the Buddha resided. Eagerly,
she approached the Seat of the Buddhas where the Teacher sat. "I
wish to have medicine for my son, Exalted One," she said.

Smiling serenely, the Buddha answered: "It is well that you have
come here. This is what you must do. You must go to each house
in the city, one by one, and from each you must seek to fetch tiny
grains of mustard seed. But not just any house will do. You must
only take mustard seeds from those houses in which no one has ever
died."

Gotami agreed at once and delightedly set out to reenter the city.
At the first house she knocked and asked, saying: "It is I, Gotami,
sent by the Possessor of the Ten Forces. You are to give me tiny

grains of mustard seed. This is the medicine I must have for my son." And when they brought her the mustard seed, she added: "Before I take the seed, tell me, is this a house in which no one has died?" "Oh no, Gotami," they answered, "the dead from this house are beyond counting." "Then I must go elsewhere," said Gotami; "the Exalted One was very clear about this. I am to seek out mustard seeds only from those houses which death has not visited."

On she went from one house to the next. But always the answer was the same. In the entire city there was no house which death had not touched. Finally she understood why she had been sent on this hopeless mission. She left the city, overcome with her feelings, and carried her dead son to the burning-ground. There she gave him up.

Returning to the monastery, she was greeted by the softly smiling Buddha who asked her: "Good Gotami, did you fetch the tiny grains of mustard seed from the house without death, as I told you to?"

And Gotami answered: "Most honored sir, there are no houses where death is not known. All mankind is touched by death. My own dear son is dead. But I see now that whoever is born must die. Everything passes away. There is no medicine for this but acceptance of it. There is no cure but the knowing. My search for the mustard seeds is over. You, O Possessor of the Ten Forces, have given me refuge. Thank you, my Exalted One."

During the lifetime of the Buddha as he walked among his disciples, his followers did not separate out his person from his teachings. His own way of being and his relationship to those who came to him was so much a part of his teachings that to believe in him was to grasp his doctrines. However, once he was gone, the teaching that remained became hollow. His followers could repeat from memory what he had taught, but their connection with the person of the Teacher was gradually lost.[2]

THE MASTER OF THE TAO

Indian Buddhism became more and more speculative over the years following Buddha's death. As these, by now, not so useful teachings moved north into China, they encountered the Taoism of Lao Tzu (605 B.C.) and Chuang Tzu (330 B.C.), and became transformed into the often humorous, tradition-defying, ultimately practical approach that would later emerge as Zen.

Who was this Chuang Tzu, and what then is the Tao? Not so easy to answer such inquiries. In ancient China, philosophers and sages of many different schools were all concerned with a single central question: How is a man to live in a chaotic, absurd world, dominated by human suffering? The answer to this question offered by the Taoist Master Chuang Tzu was: "Free yourself from the world."[3]

This freeing had not to do with denial of reality or flight from it. Rather freedom lies in achieving *wu-wei*, a state of inaction, without striving, a state in which one merges with the Tao, the Way of Life, that underlying unity of man, Nature, and the Universe. But Chuang Tzu did not explain this to his followers; he showed them the Way through parables, funny stories, or fables, thus: There was once a one-legged dragon named Kui, whose envy of a centipede led him to ask, "How can you possibly manage a hundred legs, when I manage my one leg with difficulty?" "It is so simple," replied the centipede. "I do not manage them at all. They land all over the place like drops of spit."[4]

Each man must learn then to live as the accomplished artisan works, skillfully, with grace, and without having to stop and think out what is to be done at each point. Each man must start out by becoming who he is. Each creature has its own special gifts. "Fine horses can travel a hundred miles a day, but they cannot catch mice."[5]

When a worried man came to visit the Taoist Master Lao Tzu in hope of being relieved of his problems, the Master immediately asked, "Why did you come with all this crowd of people?" Whirling around to see who was standing by him, the worried man found no one. What the Master had referred to, of course, was the burdensome company of conventional concepts of good and bad, and the like, which each man carries with him—that "crowd of people" who constitute our needless worries. Each man can forsake his man-made ills if he will only give up his habit of labeling things as good or evil. Thus Chuang Tzu tells us the parable of the woman with leprosy, who, "when she gives birth to a child in the deep of the night, rushes to fetch a torch and examine it, trembling with terror lest it look like herself."[6]

It is the striving after those things which are not really our own nature, rather than giving ourselves over to the Way, that costs us our happiness. But the Taoist Masters knew that this was not something easily taught, especially when the learner depended on logical debate as a way of establishing the truth. And so the Master did not offer logical arguments. Instead he told funny, sometimes absurd stories to free those who came to learn from him, to help them to see that they would never find happiness until they stopped looking for it. Here is an example of such an exchange:

Hui Tzu said to Chuang Tzu, "I have a big tree named ailanthus. Its trunk is too gnarled and bumpy to apply a measuring line to, its branches too bent and twisty to match up to a compass or square. You could stand it by the road and no carpenter would look twice at it. Your words, too, are big and useless, and so everyone alike spurns them!"

Chuang Tzu said, "Maybe you've never seen a wildcat or a weasel. It crouches down and hides, watching for something to come along. It leaps and races east and west, not hesitating to go high or low—until it falls into the trap and dies in the net. Then again there's the yak, big as a cloud covering the sky. It certainly knows how to be big, though it doesn't know how to catch rats. Now you have this big tree and you're distressed because it's useless. Why don't you plant it in Not-Even-Anything Village, or the field of Broad-and-Boundless, relax and do nothing by its side, or lie down for a free and easy sleep under it? Axes will never shorten its life, nothing can ever harm it. If there's no use for it, how can it come to grief or pain?"[7]

There is so much worrying over whether a man is one thing or another, whether he is in one place or another. So much of a man goes into making needless distinctions, when transformations need not bother us so long as they free a man to lose himself in the Tao, just as all a fish needs is to get lost in the water. So it was with Chuang Chou, who one night dreamed that he was a butterfly. He was so happy flitting and fluttering from one flower to another, gliding gently on warm breezes, and watching the bright sunlight being beautifully transformed by the lovely colors of his translucent wings. He was so wonderfully a butterfly that he no longer knew he was Chuang Chou. In the morning when he awoke, the dream still seemed so real that he did not know if he was a man who had dreamed he was a butterfly, or a butterfly who was now dreaming that he was a man.[8]

Thus, the Masters of the Tao teach that life can best be understood, metaphorically, as a totally free and purposeless journey. Even death need not change things, for it too is part of the Way. And so:

When Lao Tzu died, Ch'in Shih went to mourn for him; but after giving three cries, he left the room.

"Weren't you a friend of the Master?" asked Lao Tzu's disciples.

"Yes."

"And you think it's all right to mourn him this way?"

"Yes," said Ch'in Shih. "At first I took him for a real man, but now I know he wasn't. A little while ago, when I went in to mourn, I found old men weeping for him as though they were weeping for a son, and young men weeping for him as though they were weeping for a mother. To have gathered a group like *that*, he must have done something to make them talk about him, though he didn't ask them to talk, or make them weep for him, though he didn't ask them to weep. This is to hide from Heaven, turn your back on the true state of affairs, and forget what you were born with. In the old days, this was called the crime of hiding from Heaven. Your master happened to come because it was his time, and he happened to leave because things follow along. If you are content with the time and willing to follow along, then grief and joy have no way to enter in. In the old days, this was called being freed from the bonds of God.

"Though the grease burns out of the torch, the fire passes on, and no one knows where it ends."[9]

When Chuang Tzu discovered that his disciples were planning a splendid funeral for him, he demanded to know why they wasted themselves in this way when, if he went unburied, he would have all of heaven and earth, of stars and planets about him. His disciples protested that if he remained above ground, he would surely be eaten by crows and kites. And the Master of the Tao replied: "Well, above ground I shall be eaten by crows and kites and below it by ants and worms. In either case I shall be eaten. Why are you so partial to birds?"[10]

The Masters of the Tao understood that it was not so easy for each man to lose himself in the Way. They offered two seemingly contradictory alternatives to being stuck with those self-defeating struggles that keep a man from being at one with his own nature. The first solution is offered to a man who keeps trying to attain the unattainable (the gift of the Tao), a man who persists in trying to get what effort cannot attain, a man who persists in reasoning about things that cannot be understood. He is warned that he will be destroyed by the very thing that he seeks. He is advised that the right beginning for him is to stop trying when he can get no further by his own actions. The first solution is to give up.

Useless conflict with the unchangeable laws of existence simply wears a man out. So, too, if he struggles against aspects of his own nature that do not yield. And so for some men the first solution, the solution of giving up, does not work. Such men turn then to the second solution, the solution of giving in. And so it is told:

When Price Mou of Wei was living as a hermit in Chungsan, he said to the Taoist Chuang Tzu, "My body is here amid lakes and streams; but my heart is in the palace of Wei. What am I to do?" "Care more for what you have in yourself," said Chuang Tzu, "and less for what you can get from others." "I know I ought to," said the prince, "but I cannot get the better of my feelings." "If you cannot get the better of your feelings," replied Chuang Tzu, "then give play to them. Nothing is worse for the soul than struggling not to give play to feeling that it cannot control. This is called the Double Injury, and of those that sustain it, none live out their natural span."[11]

If you cannot give up, give in.

Men often resist both kinds of advice. Now, as then, men are most interested in sustaining the illusions of control and certainty. To this end, men organize and tamper as though they know at each point what is best and how things should be. The Masters of the Tao taught that to organize is to destroy. We must discover the natural order of things, rather than try to invent it. That this is clearly so is shown in this tale:

Fus, the god of the Southern Ocean, and Fret, the god of the Northern Ocean, happened once to meet in the realm of Chaos, the god of the center. Chaos treated them handsomely, and they discussed together what they could do to repay his kindness. They had noticed that, whereas everyone else has seven apertures, for sight, hearing, eating, breathing, and so on, Chaos had none. So they decided to make the experiment of boring holes in him. Every day they bored a hole, and on the seventh day Chaos died.[12]

Taoism did not remain the powerful mystical yielding to which the Masters of the Tao had first pointed. The idea of letting go of logic, control, and organization without knowing what one is passively getting into was not easily tolerated by most people. It was so much easier to have a positive program, clear methodology, and certain goals that as Taoism became more popular, it degenerated. Eventually this subtly provocative, elusive, but freeing vision was reduced to an "amalgam of superstition, alchemy, magic, and health-culture."[13]

THE TEACHER OF ETHICS

The wisdom of Confucius, the Teacher of Ethics, and that of the Masters of the Tao arose in China at about the same time (about 2,500 years ago), and at times served as rival ways of life for the people of that time and place. The Taoists taught that organization destroys natural order. They taught inaction, an absence of striving, and encouraged each man to give himself passively over to the Way. They taught this largely by catching up their students in absurdly funny stories, which were often both irrational and iconoclastic.

The Teachers of Ethics, on the other hand, taught the necessity of a well-reasoned social order based on each man's personal cultivation of an ethical approach. This attitude was to be centered on a consideration of the feelings of other people. Although respect for authority and the study of the writings of the ancients were also stressed, this was also to be a reasoned approach that took current needs into account, rather than being some blind, unthinking obedience. Thus these Teachers of Ethics set out actively to change the social order to a more humanistic approach. No divine ideal was needed. The measure of man was, from then on, to be man himself.

The Teachers of Ethics taught with more directness than did the Masters of the Tao. They taught by admonishing others about moral issues and by having the Teacher himself set an example of high moral idealism. The exemplary manner of the Confucianist Teachers known as *Ju* is described as follows. In preparation for dealing with requests for advice, the Teacher was to begin by cultivating the required knowledge independently, at the same time attempting to develop the integrity and honesty of his character. His whole person must bear the stamp of his philosophy, from the orderliness of his dress to the great care that is evident in his actions.

. . . his great refusals seem like lack of respect and his little refusals seem like false manners; when he appears on public occasions, he looks awe-inspiring, and on small occasions he appears self-retiring; his services are difficult to get and difficult to keep while he appears gentle and weak. . . . (He) may be approached by gentle manners but may not be cowed by force; he is affable but he cannot be made to do what he doesn't want; and he may be killed, but may not be humiliated. . . . (He) lives with the moderns but studies with the ancients. . . . His life may be threatened, but the course of his conduct may not be changed. Although he lives in danger, his soul remains his own, and even then he does not forget the sufferings of the people.[14]

The basic method of these Teachers of Ethics was conversational, resulting in the remaining collections of sayings (the *Analects*). But the sayings are a bit misleading, as suggested by the nature of the dialogue between Teacher and disciple implied in Confucius' statement: "I won't teach a man who is not anxious to learn, and will not explain to one who is not trying to make things clear to himself. And if I explain one-fourth and the man doesn't go back and reflect and think out the implications in the remaining three-fourths for himself, I won't bother to teach him again."[15]

There was also an element of highly personal devotion in these seemingly intellectual exchanges. The disciple's commitment to his

Teacher of Ethics is well stated by Yen Huei. One time he and his teacher were attacked and temporarily separated. When Yen Huei reappeared, his Teacher said, "I had thought you had been killed." Yen's answer was, "As long as you live, how dare I be killed." No less concern was shown by a Teacher who was asked why he wept at the death of one of his many disciples. He replied simply, "If I don't weep bitterly at the death of such a person, for whom else shall I weep bitterly?"

The instruction of these Teachers of Ethics transformed many individual lives and even affected whole societies when those whose characters were cultivated were noblemen and rulers. But, after a while, what had started out as dialogue about practical situations, what had been guidelines for useful conventions within which men could live in peace and harmony, all ended up as a set of codified ideals through which to achieve perfection. Eventually, if someone wanted to be a superior man, he was expected to master some 3,300 rules of conduct—becoming instead a superior actor.[16]

THE ZEN MASTERS

Scholars can trace some of the steps in the evolution of Zen Buddhism from its earliest antecedents in the "pure" Theravada Buddhism of Southern India many centuries ago. They can follow its course as its ways caught the imagination of more and more people, in Northern India, then on into China, and finally into Japan. Doctrinal changes and permutations of style can be understood in the light of changing interactions as early Buddhism was affected by the emerging social, political, and cultural patterns to which these beliefs were subjected in going from one group of converts to another.

However, there is a simpler and more Zen history of Zen Buddhism. It goes like this. It happened that one time a very important personage came to the Buddha for enlightenment. This nobleman offered the Buddha a golden blossom and requested that in return the Buddha should preach to him of the meaning of reality. The Enlightened One took the flower in his hand, held it up before him, and gazed at it without speaking. After a while, the nobleman smiled. He had received enlightenment. It was this smile of enlightenment that was then passed down from one teacher to the next. Thus did Zen arise, and thus did it endure.[17]

This story of the Buddha's showing the way to enlightenment without speaking a word is an important example of one kind of technique of Zen instruction[18]—the direct method. By relying on action rather than on words, the Zen Master draws the pupil into being with each fleeting moment of life, as it is, without time to build ideas out of words or to use memory to make *now* into a part of the familiar past.

Traditionally, the Zen Master carries a wooden staff with which he can cut through the philosophizing of his pupil by striking him sharply and unexpectedly on the side of the head, often at the same time loudly crying out, "Kwats!" Neither the blow nor the cry "mean" anything. They simply bring the pupil quickly and clearly back into the present, without explanation or hope of explanation, for there is nothing to be explained. Reflection about life must not be confused with life itself. Life is to live. If I point with my finger at the moon, it would be a great mistake for you to stare at my finger and to believe that now you had come to know the moon.

Although this direct method of wordless instruction is the teaching technique most uniquely characteristic of the ways of the Zen Masters, they do use verbal methods as well. Perhaps the best known of these is the Koan Exercise. A koan is a problem which the Master gives to his disciple. The disciple tries to solve it in conventional or intellectual ways until he realizes he cannot. At that point he may become "enlightened" or fall into despair.

The koan may consist of a statement made or a question asked by the Zen Master, such as: "Tell me the sound of one hand clapping"; or "Show me your original face before you were born"; or "The flower is not red, nor is the willow green."

Sometimes the koan consists of an answer by the Zen Master, given in response to a question posed by the disciple, such as this:

The young monk asks, "Who is the Buddha?" The Master replies, "Three grains of rice."

The young monk asks, "What is the secret of enlightenment?" The Master replies, "When you are hungry, eat; and when you are tired, sleep."

The young monk asks, "What is Zen?" The Master replies, "Boiling oil over a blazing fire."

The young monk asks, "How shall I see the truth?" The Master replies, "Through your everyday eyes."

The Koan may seem straightforward in tone, or it may be openly bewildering. It always turns out to be paradoxical, impenetrable by logic. The disciple may spend months or even years trying to solve the problem, until it occurs to him that there is no problem to be solved. The only "solution" is to give up trying to "understand" (be-

cause there is nothing to be understood) and to respond spontaneously. Enlightenment consists in recognizing that the Zen Master has
nothing to teach. The disciple already knows all there is to know,
but he does not trust his spontaneous perception of the world. He
insists that there must be more to it, something beyond his experience,
some secret to be discovered. In this way he creates problems much
like the survival problem of a man who has his hands clutched tightly
around his own throat.

The nature of the Zen Master's non-teaching and of where he stands
in relation to his disciples is most charmingly apparent in the anec-
dotes which make up the wealth of Zen writings. For example, there
was a young disciple of the Zen Master, Bankei. One day he complained of having an ungovernable temper and asked how he could
cure it. Bankei allowed as how that was very strange indeed and
said, "Let me see what you have." The young man replied that he
could not show it to the master just then. Bankei wanted to know
when the student would be able to show his temper to him. The
student could not tell him anything more than that the temper arose
unexpectedly. Bankei concluded, "Then it must not be your own true
nature. If it were, you could show it to me anytime. When you were
born you did not have it, and your parents did not give it to you.
Think that over."[19]

For some seekers, enlightenment is instantaneous. So it was with
the young monk in search of enlightenment who came to the monastery in which the Zen Master Joshu resided. He approached Joshu
the first day, saying to the old man, "Please teach me." In response
Joshu asked, "Have you eaten your rice porridge?" "Yes, I have eaten
my rice porridge," replied the young monk. "Then you had better
wash your bowl," said Joshu. The young monk smiled, knowing that
at that moment he had become enlightened.[20]

In a way, the Zen Master shows that not only does he have nothing
to teach, but also that there is nothing to learn. All is just as it appears
to be. It is only the questioning that creates the problems, only the
demand for order, for secret meaning, and for certainty. Yet, though
enlightenment is always imminent, it sometimes comes only by way
of long years of asceticism, meditation, and disciplined study with
a Zen Master.

So it was with Shoju, who had studied long years with the old
Zen Master Mu-nan, to whom he was to be the sole successor. When
Mu-nan believed he would die soon, he called Shoju to his side.
Because Shoju was the only one who would carry on Mu-nan's teach-
ings, the old man offered his disciple a valuable book which tradi-

tionally had been passed down to represent succession. Shoju protested:

"If the book is such an important thing, you had better keep it. . . . I received your Zen without writing and am satisfied with it as it is."
"I know that," said Mu-nan. "Even so, this work has been carried from master to master for seven generations, so you may keep it as a symbol of having received the teaching. Here."
The two happened to be talking before a brazier. The instant Shoju felt the book in his hands, he thrust it into flaming coals. He had no lust for possessions. Mu-nan, who had never been angry before, yelled: "What are you doing!"
Shoju shouted back: "What are you saying!"[21]

Interest in Zen has become subject to two seemingly opposite types of corruption, recently characterized as Beat Zen and Square Zen.

Beat Zen is a kind of indiscriminate justification of anything that occurs by accident or caprice. Such acts and happenings are seen as being more real, artistic, or free than anything that comes of discipline or design. This devotion to randomness is a far cry from the controlled accidents of Zen artists and the simple asceticism of the old Zen Masters. Beat Zen is easy Zen, phony Zen, born of rebelliousness, colored by Bohemian affectations, and often mediated by drug experiences.

Square Zen, on the other hand, is cultist, an esoteric discipline that says that enlightenment can only be achieved in the way a particular group prescribes (such as by spending stipulated periods in special meditation positions in a Zen monastery). Devotees are highly conscious of degrees of initiation, preoccupied with ritual, and burdened with the difficulty of what they are about. This group seems to have lost the original Zen qualities of naturalness, spontaneity, and the multiplicity of paths to enlightenment.

8 Metaphors from Ancient Greece and Rome

THE SAGE

About the sixth century B.C. in ancient Greece, there was a great deal of the anxiety and unrest that are born of the radical achievement of a gifted people. The development of democratic constitutions required passionate struggles. Independent judgments and opinions were out in the political arena, and the impact of the individual personalities of many men became increasingly important.

At about the same time, there began to emerge a radically new way of looking at the problems of man in nature. As philosophers reexamined the problem of origins, they moved away from thinking in terms of "the beginning," of the time when the world was created.[1] Instead they began thinking in terms of a "ground of existence," a "first cause." Never mind "Who made the world and why?" Rather, they began to ask, "What is fundamental in the universe?" These thinkers boldly assumed that there was a single underlying order to a universe which could now be viewed as an intelligible unity.

This was, then, a time when old ties to faith and unexamined morals were strongly shaken. It was a time of "the emancipation of thought from myth."[2] The moral direction of everyday life was threatened, and the ethical direction of the young was uncertain. Perhaps it was in part in response to this need for moral guidance that a small band of teachers arose who have come to be called the Seven Wise Men of Greece, or by some, the Seven Sages of Greece. This band is usually said to include Bias, Chilon, Cleobulus, Periander, Pittacus, Solon, and Thales.

These teachers were usually engaged in public life, but this seems to have been more a matter of their own desire for understanding and impact than as a response to the demand of their communities. The Sages taught in Sparta and in Crete, but their influence was underplayed outside of those places. The reason was, in part, that it was more politic for a community to pretend ignorance before its neighbors, to be thought to rule by bravery and power than to be known to rule by wisdom.

And so it was that these Sages met privately with their students and that the students were to hide what they had learned from any foreigner with whom they might come into contact. We learn from Socrates that these primitive philosophers taught in a way that allowed their pupils "at any point in the discourse . . . [to] be darting out some notable saying, terse and full of meaning, with unerring aim; and the person with whom he is talking seems to be like a child in his hands."[3]

Few of these "short memorable sentences" have come down to us, though it is one such homily which is the pivot of Socrates' dialogue with the Sophist, Protagoras. Together they pick at the saying of the Sage, Pittacus, "Hard it is to be good." This allows Plato a device for examining the question of whether or not virtue can be taught.

Two other sayings of the Sages have been preserved—no, not preserved, but rather enshrined. These mottoes came to be inscribed on the temple of the Oracle of Delphi, the temple of the cult of Apollo. It was to this place that Greeks so long came for counsel. The saying of the Sages read: "Know thyself." It was a phrase which was to "become the central touchstone for psychotherapy ever since."[4] If this injunction toward self-knowledge seemed a discouraging burden, the Sages added: "Nothing too much."

The Sages began as primitive philosophers, as men who worked with the problem of illuminating the young and of offering moral guidance and encouragement for ethical reflection. Eventually, however, later in the history of the temple of Apollo, their teachings were used to support humility before the gods. No longer a source of support in an intelligible universe, their teachings then became the mottoes of caution by which men could avoid divine vengeance (*nemesis*), which might be unleashed against those guilty of the arrogant presumption of being able to know the world (*hubris*).

THE ORACLE

There had been at first a time during which the temple of Apollo was the site of much helpful counsel to the people of Greece. It was here that Apollo, the god of healing (whose son Aesculapius became patron saint of medicine), spoke as an Oracle. Those who came for help heard him speak through his priestess in the same sense that spirits are said to speak through a latter-day medium at a séance.

Many troubled people journeyed to that shrine on the plateau of the mountains at Delphi. It is believed that a great number of these petitioners came, not with personal psychological problems, but rather with the anxiety of men living in radically changing times. The social and political order was in a state of ferment; even the structure of the family was crumbling. It was a time of emergence of new and unpredictable forces, and men were faced with having to struggle individually with the *"anxiety of new possibilities."*[5] Apollo, as the god of form, reason, and logic, could assure them of purpose behind the seeming chaos.

A Greek man, making the two-day walk from Athens to the shrine of the Oracle, would have time to concentrate on his problems, perhaps to see them in the promise of a new light. At the same time he would be dreaming of how he would be helped by the Oracle, building his hopes, strengthening his faith, already playing a part in his own cure.

There was a great deal of secrecy preserved as to just what went on in the temple, and little reliable information is available as to the source of advice. It is believed that, like the sayings of later mediums, the statements made by the Oracle's priestess were somewhat cryptic and poetic, at times even vague. The troubled person who sought help had to interpret what was "really" meant. This made it possible for him to find what he was after by reading the needed meaning into the puzzling message. This could then afford the same sort of help that a man may receive by finding truth in a dream, the same truth that he would find it so very difficult to take full responsibility for as a part of a waking thought.

And so for a long while this shrine of Apollo, this temple of the Oracle of Delphi, served as a source of monumental reassurance to the troubled people of Greece. Here they could find omniscience in a time of uncertainty and personal counsel in a time of failing social structures. Here a man could learn how to bring his tumultuous feelings into harmony with the form and constructive order that he sought. He was offered support in living a life of "controlled passion." Only later, as some of the Greek teachers became increasingly afraid of the power of driving passions, did the shrine of the Oracle come to operate as a source of inhibition and repression.

THE MAD GOD

It is not possible to understand the role of the Oracle for the worshippers of Apollo without also looking into the other face of Greek paganism, the cult of Dionysus, the Mad God. If Apollo is the god of self-control and moderation, then Dionysus is the god of frenzy and abandon. One was the spirit and the other the flesh, as they vied for who would be the more important influence in the daily life of Greece. The ancient Greeks sometimes said, "Apollo is the head but he needs a body," but modern Greeks have been known to point out that "you don't need Apollo in the bedroom."[6]

Apollo is said to have come to Delphi riding on the back of a dolphin. There he is said to have slain the sacred Python with his arrows of the sun, his arrows of light, purity, and truth. The Python had lived at the center of the earth, the *omphalos* or navel of Delphi, and so his slaying by Apollo represented the victory of the higher sphere of the sky over the baser earth. It is Apollo who brings "light, artistic inspiration, and beauty . . ., [who is] objective, calm, aloof, universal, unifying, and ordered."[7] No wonder that he brings sunlight to vanquish crudity and disorder.

Dionysus, in contrast, is the reckless, willful, self-perpetuating biological urge, a force of irrational, blind impetuousness. It is no surprise that his emergence is more sordid, more filled with turmoil. The Mad God was the half-divine, half-human product of the adulterous union of Zeus with the mortal woman, Semele.

Hera, the jealously enraged wife of Zeus, could not hurt him directly. Instead, she made his lover wonder whether she was being courted by some monster in disguise. Semele would not make love to Zeus unless he proved that he really was the king of the gods. Zeus appeared to her in all his glory, complete with lightning and thunder, only to consume her in flames from his lightning bolts. Poor Semele was pregnant at the time, but Zeus was able, at the last moment, to snatch the unborn Dionysus from the divine fire of his mother. He sewed him up in his thigh, from which he was later born.

Dionysus thrived as a baby. When a new vine grew out of those which formed his cradle, he and the nymphs who raised him tasted of the fruit of the vine. They all found song, dance, laughter, and happy intoxication. Hera, still furious and unforgiving, eventually drove Dionysus mad, and he roamed the world spreading frenzied joy, intoxication with life, and the madness of creative abandonment.

This Mad God came to represent both sexual fertility and the growth of all the fruits of the earth. Spring festivals were held in his honor, in which he took the form of a snake, a bull, a goat, and was symbolized by a great erect phallus. But too, he was the violent destroyer who came in the form of fire, of a panther, a lion, and a lynx.

At best, "Dionysus epitomized and incarnated the ambivalence and wild spirit of human emotions: love and hate, life and death, creation and destruction, tragedy and comedy. He balanced these antitheses."[8]

If Apollo brought reassuring reason, order, and objectivity to the Greeks, Dionysus brought the divine madness of inspired creativity, the freedom of blessed ecstasy, and the deliverance of lusty sexuality. He turned the people he inspired toward the life of the flesh, of free expression, of pleasure touched with madness.

Later when this cult of the Mad God appeared in Rome, it became debased into celebration by orgies of debauchery, rather than simple revelry. At these Bacchanalia, the most decadent met to plot crimes and political conspiracies. Where once there had been freedom from the oppression of too much goodness and order, now there was only evil for its own sake.

THE MIDWIFE

Fortunately, the virtues of the Apollonian way had not been all lost along the way. Socrates, for one, was much given to finding ways to educate men to the good, particularly by means of dialogue. In a discussion with Theatetus,[9] Socrates suggests the metaphor of the midwife as a way of communicating just what it is that he does when he teaches younger men. Socrates reveals the secret that he is the son of a "brave and burly" midwife named Phaenarete, and that he himself is a practitioner of midwifery. Not knowing that he is a midwife, most of the world sees him as merely being "the strangest of mortals . . . [who] drive[s] men to their wits' end" with his endless questions.

He points out that Artemis, the goddess of childbirth, is not herself a mother. This makes her sympathetic to others who are like her, but yet she does not honor barren women by making them midwives. This she could not do "because human nature cannot know the mystery of an art without experience." And so, by way of compromise, Artemis assigned the office of midwife to women who are old enough to be past the age of conceiving and bearing children of their own.

So it is with Socrates, himself too old to create and produce his own new ideas. Instead, he is midwife to the ideas of others. True, it is men he attends rather than women, and it is their souls that are in labor rather than their bodies. Still he believes that it is fruitful to extend the analogy of the midwife to the teacher. Thus, he finds that he knows best who is pregnant (with an idea) and who is not. The triumph of his art he describes as occurring in his "thoroughly examining whether the thought which the mind of the young man brings forth is a false idol or a noble and true birth."

Some young men who come to him "apparently have nothing in them." It is then that Socrates must "coax them into marrying someone." That is, he must lead them into relationships that will stimulate them to become creative. Not just any marriage will do. The midwife is also a most "cunning matchmaker . . . [who has] a thorough knowledge of what unions are likely to produce a brave brood."

And should a young man be pregnant with an idea when he comes to be taught by Socrates, or should he become so through his teacher's matchmaking, then Socrates, the midwife, knows how to induce labor, how "to arouse the pangs and to soothe them." The midwife goes on to help in the delivery, but it must be remembered that the child is not his. So it is that those who converse with Socrates profit from being with him. Still, he insists that they never really learn anything from him. He merely helps them to discover the ideas already growing within them. Of course, he does reserve the right to inspect the fetus and to watch for signs of deformity. Then if he thinks fit, as the midwife he "can smother the embryo in the womb." He asks that the young men do not quarrel with him over such judgments of their conceptions, but, he points out, "there are some who were ready to bite me when I deprived them of a darling folly."

At his best, Socrates is that enabling midwife to the birthing of other men's ideas. At worst, his whole approach seems a put-on. The clearest example of this is the unconvincing dialogue in which Socrates uses Meno's slave as a foil, leading him through paces that are intended to demonstrate that he already possessed an inherent knowledge of mathematics. The reader gets the impression that Socrates demonstrates only how well he can manipulate a willing victim into saying what he wants him to say. What reason do we have to believe that virtue was more heroic or frailty less mean in ancient Greece than at any other time or place in man's history?

THE MONITOR

The people of ancient Greece and ancient Rome struggled, as men have always struggled, with the problem of living in a world filled with disappointments, with pain, and with suffering. What is a man to make of a life so much made up of evil, a life over which he seems to have so little mastery, a life so irreversible and so fleeting? One of the solutions which was proposed in ancient Greece was that of the Epicureans. Epicurus equated good with pleasure, and pain with evil, but he realized that simple hedonism often led to more pain than pleasure in the long run. He proposed instead that a wiser man would cut down on his desires, become highly selective in the pleasures he pursued, and live a simple temperate life.

A very different and more complex set of precepts were proposed by the Stoics of ancient Greece and Rome. Stoic philosophy includes the writings of several philosophers (such as Epictetus, Marcus Aurelius, Seneca, and Zeno), which appeared over a span of almost five hundred years (three centuries before Christ to two centuries after Christ). The ideas differ depending on who is writing, or even on where a particular Stoic philosopher was in his own development.

There are certain central themes to Stoicism (though they may receive different emphasis at different points). Stoic philosophers urged every man to live according to Nature and to depend on Reason to help him to find his proper place in Nature. The Stoics were telling each man that he might as well accept things as they come. A man can try to change those things that he has the power to change, but Reason tells him that most events that befall a man are immutable determinations of a rationally ordered state of Nature. If some event seems evil, it only appears to be so because man is not wise enough to understand its place in the natural order of the world.

In any case, nothing's to be done about it. It simply makes no sense to fret and worry over matters that we are totally helpless to influence one way or the other. In ways such as this, the Stoics tried to teach useful ideas on how to live a happy, constructive life without being destroyed by the world. And, unlike the Epicureans who tended to preach withdrawal from the world into a simpler life, the Stoics urged active participation in the social and political life of the community. They encouraged men toward helpful involvement with others, but only in the manner of a disinterested, dispassionate brotherhood-of-men.

This matter of being dispassionate is crucial to the Stoic way of meeting life's many frustrations, disappointments, losses, and betrayals. Emotion must give way to the constraint of will. Self-control of heroic proportion is the keystone on which Stoic acceptance of life depends. But how is a man to be able to pursue a life which is not dominated by longing, by sorrow, or by anger?

If a man is weak, he may need someone to admonish him. Certainly, even a stronger man may need direction during the early development of his moral character. Indeed, every man is sometimes careless and at such times needs a guardian to tug at his sleeve and to call attention to what he has overlooked. And even the very best and wisest of men may need counsel and support in the face of temptation, or when beset by great losses.[10]

What is needed is a Monitor, a counselor who will set down precepts by which other men may be guided. During the first century A.D., there lived such a man in Rome, a Stoic philosopher named Lucius Annaeus Seneca. This Seneca provided such guidance for other men in the form of letters and moral essays. These originated as personal words of advice, of praise and criticism, of exhortation and consolation, which were addressed to relatives and personal friends. Later some of these thoughts were expanded into more philosophical treatises.

Some of the general counsel offered by the Monitor Seneca is to be found in his essay, "On Providence." He will not pretend that there is but little hardship for a man to face, for "uphill and downhill must he go, be tossed about, and guide his bark through stormy waters; he must keep his course in spite of fortune. Much that is hard, much that is rough will befall him, but he himself will soften the one, and make the other smooth."[11]

Can a man protect himself by aspiring to virtue? Not so simple a question:

Why . . . does God sometimes allow evil to befall good men? Assuredly, he does not. . . . [He] keeps them far from . . . sin and crime, evil counsel and schemes for greed, blind lust and avarice. . . . [It is true that even] good men lose their sons . . . are sent into exile . . . [and] are slain. . . . Why do they suffer certain hardships? Is it that they may teach others to endure them; [that] they were born to be a pattern.[?][12]

All that a good man can do is to "offer himself to Fate." Even good men make too much of death, an end to suffering, which can come so swiftly. Not only need death not be dreaded, it can even be welcomed. In fact, if a man knows how to die, fortune has no power over him. Thus, suicide becomes a desirable way out of situations that are completely intolerable (situations such as slavery).

Seneca writes about other Stoic issues such as banishing anger from the mind, responding with mercy, the meaning of giving and of receiving, and the shortness of life. The important issue is to get on with living it, rather than to sit around and bemoan it.

As a Monitor of the spirit, the most vivid function for Seneca is that of offering consolation to the bereaved. His literature of consolation consists of comfort and advice addressed to particular others, but also having meaning for the many. For instance, he writes one consoling essay to Marcia, a woman of Rome whose father has killed himself in an act of political defiance, and who has endured the death of her four sons as well.

Another essay of consolation is directed to Polybius, an admired Roman official who is grieving over the death of his brother. The third of Seneca's consolations is addressed to his own mother, Helvia, in an effort to comfort her about her mourning his being in exile in Corsica.

Seneca's approach is thoughtful, considerate, even tender, as when he tells Helvia he hopes that "even though I could not stop your weeping, I had meanwhile at least wiped away your tears."[13]

At the same time he puts forward the tough-mindedness of the Stoic Monitor when he goes on to point out: "Someone will say: 'What sort of consolation is this, to recall ills that are blotted out and to set the mind, when it is scarcely able to bear one sorrow, in full view of all its sorrows?' . . . my purpose will be not to heal by gentle measures, but to cauterize and cut."[14]

He patiently attempts to take the mourner through all of the alternatives which Reason provides. He helps the one he is consoling to see that "nothing is everlasting, few things are even long-lasting."[15] Further, he points out how things might have been worse. He offers examples of the different ways other people have responded to losses and just what the results have been. He cajoles, coerces, supports, and harasses.

Yet, ironically, perhaps the most significant function he performs is that he writes at length about what they are suffering through, taking the mourner through the whole experience in depth. Though he may suggest that grief that cannot ultimately be overcome should be hidden, still, he points out that "to share one's grief with many is in itself a kind of consolation."[16] And though he points out that life is too brief to waste on sorrow, he also assures the mourner that his goal is to help her to "conquer," not to "minimize" her sadness and pain.

Thus the Stoic attitude can be very helpful when one is powerless to do anything else. However, this same acceptance of so much that happens as a determination of Nature encourages acquiescence to avoidable evils. And too, the attempt to avoid situations that might lead to disappointment and strong feelings of sorrow may dispose men to avoid the risks that lead to adventure, to freedom, and to joy.

9 *Metaphors from the Renaissance*

The Renaissance is usually described as having begun in Italy around 1300 A.D. and then spread northward across Europe manifesting itself in England by the seventeenth century. Like other historical categories, it is, of course, an academic invention aimed at bringing the appearance of order to the stubbornly uncontrollable sprawl of history. And just as with other arbitrary conceptual conventions, it is useful only so long as we do not mistake it for reality. Therefore, it is important to understand that whatever phenomena we attribute to it, the Renaissance begins before and extends beyond this arbitrary slice through time.

Even so, what then is meant by the Renaissance? The Renaissance (literally the "rebirth") is a period of reemergence of learning and the arts, after a period called the Middle Ages or Dark Ages, during which such human productions had allegedly disappeared. This historical category is, of course, quite as arbitrary and misleading as any other. Nonetheless, there was something in the wind, and times were indeed changing (though not so discretely as such categories suggest).

During the Middle Ages, men had lived in a tightly ordered world, run by God, dominated by Christian symbols, administered by a single Mother Church, and policed by feudal lords. Europe was the world, earth was the center of the universe, and what those men believed was certain.

The rediscovery of the classics during the Renaissance was to be very important in changing all of this. More and more, the translation and study of long-neglected Greek and Roman writings became a source of excitement and renewal. In Renaissance painting, sculpture, and writing, the rediscovered classical characters, ideas, and symbols began to appear with increasing frequency.

By itself, this phenomenon would have opened up new ways of seeing the world; but there was something more subtle afoot. In the name of Beauty, classical symbols appeared side by side with hitherto unquestioned Christian images, neither being given more importance than the other. When Venus and Christ are equally valid, Christ has lost his final authority. It was during this period that the Reformation formally challenged the authority and legitimacy of the Catholic Church.

A man living during this period would have had to have had his world view shattered, would have had to experience his mind being "blown." The Renaissance was to be an age of curiosity and adventure. In addition to the classical revival's making religious, literary, and artistic boundaries more ambiguous, explorers were now finding strange lands beyond the endless seas. Not only were the seas no longer impenetrable barriers, but what was more, the world itself was not flat but round. The earth was not the center of the universe around which the sun and stars revolved, but rather this sphere had to trek around the sun. The telescope showed that not even the faithful stars had really been dependably known.

Development of the sciences also served to demythologize God's world. Supernatural explanation began to give way to a naturalistic conception, which could be perceived directly, even by the untutored, in the realistic perspective and anatomy of Renaissance drawing.

There also were social and political changes which offered supportive interplay to the changing cosmology. The little worlds of feudalism began to become consolidated into strong national governments ruled by kings. During the same period, a new middle class of merchants and bankers was coming to power.

Before this, a man had known where he stood, what the world was about, and where it ended. Now the foundations had been shaken, and some structures overturned. Never mind one's place in God's world—now it was man who counted, and the individual man at that. What was a man to do? "Do what thou wilt," became the motto. All prior bets were off. There were no more guarantees. It was a time of freedom—freedom to search out beauty and freedom to develop oneself in all directions. At the same time, it was a time of profound uncertainty and great turmoil. To whom could a man turn for guidance at such a time? Let us explore some of the men who, through their writings, served as guides to the Renaissance man. The three representatives which I have chosen to discuss are: (1) Niccolo di Bernardo dei Machiavelli (1469–1527), Counselor of the Arts of the Lion and the Fox; (2) Baldesar Castiglione (1478–1529), Instructor in Manners; (3) Michel de Montaigne (1533–1592), Essayist of the Self. And too, there is one man who left us more legend than history, more mythical model than teachings: (4) Philippus Aurelius

Theophrastus Bombast von Hohenheim, known as Paracelsus (1490–1541), the Magus.

THE COUNSELOR IN THE ARTS
OF THE LION AND THE FOX

Niccolo di Bernardo dei Machiavelli was very much aware of the uncertainty of the Renaissance man. Now that the world was natural and consequently indefinite, it was only imperfectly knowable. No longer could one simply depend on pleasing an all-knowing and all-powerful God. Rather, a man was more stuck with his own ignorance and helplessness. Machiavelli called this new unpredictability of the natural world *fortuna*, or fortune, by which he meant chance, caprice, unpredictably changing circumstance.

Fearing he might offend the powerful Church (he eventually did), he made room for God as well when he said that "worldly events are so governed by fortune and by God, that men cannot by their prudence change them, and . . . on the contrary there is no remedy whatever."[1] Yet he was not despairing, for he believed that fortune rules only half a man's actions, and that the other half is governed by the man himself. This latter half is dependent on a man's *virtú* or virtue, by which Machiavelli meant ability.

But how is this ability to be used, with caution or with verve? Depending on the circumstances, sometimes one works, sometimes another. But all in all, Machiavelli believes, "It is better to be impetuous than cautious, for fortune is a woman, and it is necessary. if you wish to master her, to conquer her by force; and it can be seen that she lets herself be overcome by the bold rather than by those who proceed coldly."[2]

Most of the conjecture and the advice which Machiavelli offered in his writings emphasized the public rather than the private life. Still there is much implied to guide the Renaissance man in leading his private life during that period of great change.

Machiavelli was a Florentine diplomat who was fascinated by the phenomenon of power, and is sometimes thought of as the father of power politics. Of course, he did not invent the power motive, but he was an astute observer of its workings. Yet he has become known as so Satanic a cynic that his name brings a shudder, and men who coldly manipulate are said to use "a fine Italian hand."

Perhaps part of our condemning and disowning of Machiavelli has to do with our unwillingness to accept ourselves as being as nakedly power-hungry as he suggests. He acknowledges ideals and ethics, of course, but he clearly points out that "men, whether in politics, in business, or in private life, do *not* act according to their professions of virtue."[3]

He does not believe in the old images of cosmological and moral order. Man is seen as a contradiction in the universe, who is "hopelessly incontinent, infinitely desirous, [and] endlessly ambitious."[4] In his hard-headed, unsentimental way, Machiavelli does his best to face up to the reality of men's motives as he understands them.

He represents his ideas in the form of instructive discussions, the best known collections of these being *The Prince* and *The Discourses*. Typically, a section will begin with the statement of a particular thesis. This then will be followed by historical documentation aimed at supporting his contention. This approach constitutes a humanistic version of a literary tradition dating to the Middle Ages. Originally these were religious writings, called *exempla*, which described certain types of virtuous behavior that were offered as models to be imitated.

Now, what was it that Machiavelli taught the Renaissance man about the nature of human interaction and about how he might get what he wanted? He states it most clearly when he writes:

I believe it to be most true that it seldom happens that men rise from low condition to high rank without employing either force or fraud . . . a prince who wishes to achieve great things must learn to deceive. . . . Nor do I believe that there was ever a man who from obscure condition arrived at great power by merely employing open force; but there are many who have succeeded by fraud alone. . . .[5]

The advice he offers to the prince is also his advice to all men. He tells each man that he is well advised to learn how to

imitate the fox and the lion, for the lion cannot protect himself from traps, and the fox cannot protect himself from wolves. One must therefore be a fox to recognize traps, and a lion to frighten wolves. . . . If men were all good, this precept would not be a good one; but as they are bad, and would not observe their faith with you, so you are not bound to keep faith with them . . .; those that have been best able to imitate the fox have succeeded best. But it is necessary to be able to disguise this character well . . . [and] one who deceives will always find those who allow themselves to be deceived.[6]

All of this may seem heartlessly cruel and cynical. However, it is important to understand that if Machiavelli thought that overiding self-interest was society's major problem, he also believed that it held the germ of the solution as well. Man's survival, after all, would depend on some measure of restraint and renunciation of immediate gratification of his needs. It is man's very self-interest that dictates the need for maintaining an enduring state which would operate to restrict such drives. Thus when Machiavelli writes of "fraud," he does not mean deliberate deception alone. Rather, he would also include the illusions and conventions which he believes are necessary to maintaining and regulating the state. Only then can the culture survive.

Despite later response to Machiavelli's writings as the teaching of ruthless manipulation, there was no moral outcry when they first appeared. Only when the fathers of the Church began to see their position threatened by the potentially revolutionary quality of his work did they strike out against him. Only then was he condemned by the Inquisition and forced to give up his post.

Machiavelli's commitment to maintaining an enduring society has often been overlooked. Now anyone who uses Machiavelli as a guide is likely to be committed simply to doing in anyone who is in his way.

INSTRUCTOR IN MANNERS

The writings of Machiavelli served as a guide to political action, a grammar of power for the Renaissance man. *The Book of the Courtier*, by Baldesar Castiglione, was a guide to moving within the social world, a grammar of conduct. Castiglione's book is a volume of playful, social conversations which take place among the members of the Court of Urbino. This is a fictionalized, idealized court, a nostalgic vision of medieval ideals of chivalry and refinement.

For the Renaissance man set adrift in a world of uncertain standards, *The Book of the Courtier* was to become a book of manners, education, and good breeding. The ordinary illiterate had, of course, no direct contact with the writings, but standards set by "gentlemen" and the power elite had all the indirect effects they have in any age.

Castiglione attempted to elevate manners to the level of "minor morals," to the point at which there need be no distinction between behavior which is beautiful and that which is ethical. Not only is there to be no separation between what is good and what is beautiful, but the self itself is to be viewed as a work of art. The role of the courtier is to perfect himself within a perfect small society.

Castiglione proposed that there were particular attributes and attitudes that underlie the courtly ideal.[7] To begin with, what a man must seek is the harmonious development of his whole self. There is to be no expertness, no virtuosity, at the expense of leaving any important function underdeveloped. It may take discipline and concentration to do one thing fairly well, but it takes suppression of some other part of a man for him to do anything brilliantly. The courtier must seek mastery without overdevelopment. Castiglione encouraged an "amateur spirit," through which it might be necessary to sacrifice effectiveness of action to refinement of feelings.

Another important characteristic of the perfect courtier was *gravitá* a kind of relaxed dignity. He must have an unselfconscious "artless" bearing, a majestic air which is casual, almost fortuitous. This attitude will permeate his every gesture and may even be sensed in the clothes which he chooses to wear.

The most important characteristic of the perfect courtier, and perhaps the hardest to define, is *grazia*, or grace. It is not a quality that can be developed in just anyone. One must already possess the germ of it if one is to learn it. Grace is a kind of easy charm flowing from good judgment of the sort that arises in a person whose many parts are in a state of true harmony. It is an effortless giving of oneself over to whatever one does.

All of this begins to sound monumentally aristocratic when presented out of the context in which it arises. The courtly conversations. in *The Book of the Courtier* begin with the ladies and gentlemen of the Court of Urbino setting out to amuse themselves (in a way which Castiglione hopes will amuse and instruct his readers). Rather than write a series of sermons or lectures, the Instructor in Manners has his characters get together to try to decide on some games they might play. The first game proposed might be called "Each Man's Folly."[8] Because it is so much easier too see our neighbor's error than our own, one character suggests that each of them should answer the question: "If I had to be openly mad, what kind of folly would I be thought likely to display, and in what connection, going by the sparks of folly which I give out every day?" In this way the members of the court develop awareness of themselves and of the various kinds of human possibilities.

Part of this exploration of character involves the development of ideal attitudes and conduct. This search starts out in a game that could be called "The Perfect Courtier."[9] It is within this section that we learn that Castiglione is not simply concerned with an aristocratic elite, on the one hand, and a hopeless mass of dolts, on the other.

Thus, one character points out "that between such supreme grace and such absurd folly can be found a middle way, and that those who are not perfectly endowed by Nature can, through care and effort, polish and to a great extent correct their natural defects."

All in all, the Instructor in Manners turns out to be intensely interested in self-development, in which men must move toward moderation, rational balance, and flexibility. A man must be an ethical agent, but he must do so within a sense of the beautiful and with an intensely personal style. Unfortunately, this aesthetic idealism decayed in later adherents to a kind of egotism and snobbishness. The ideal of the development of the self as a work of art dedicated to harmony and moderation became a basis for shallow, foppish dilettantism.

ESSAYIST OF THE SELF

Earlier I suggested that the Renaissance man lived in a time of excitement at the cost of uncertainty, of freedom without the dependable supports of the absolute values of the Middle Ages, of unrestricted horizons for journeys yet uncharted. The writings of Machiavelli might be said to have provided him a guide to political action. Castiglione's *Book of the Courtier* offered standards of social conduct. But for help in coming to know and evaluate his personal self, he had to await the *Essays* of Michel de Montaigne.

During the Middle Ages, it would have been deemed pure folly for an ordinary man (as Montaigne claimed to be) to have wasted his life examining his own experiences. And should that ordinary man do so, he certainly would not have had the arrogance to presume that such an exploration of himself could be of any interest to anyone else. The Renaissance questioning of final authority and increased valuing of the individual served as a more likely setting, and Montaigne's work, in turn, expanded these parameters still further.

Montaigne was well versed in the classics, but he put no man's authority above the teachings of his own experience. The self and examination of its everyday experiences is the mother lode and the touchstone:

I would rather be well versed about myself than about Cicero. In the experience I have about myself I find enough to make me wise if I were a good scholar. The life of Caesar has no more of a lesson for us than our own; and whether an emperor's or an ordinary man's, it is still a life that is subject to all human accidents. Let us just listen to it: we tell ourselves all that we chiefly need.[10]

We are each, Montaigne points out, as finite as the next, no matter what our station in life. No one is exempt. Lest we be mired in our own idealizations, he notes very vividly that "both kings and philosophers defecate, and ladies too."[11] In less scatological terms, "no man is exempt from saying silly things."[12]

All in all, it is no use looking to authority when in search of truth. One must look to the self. Each man's motto must be, "What do I know?" And this must be pursued without hope of final answers. Building a rational system of answers may offer consistency, but such a system always does violence to experience.

When Montaigne turns his attention toward his self, it is not at all a matter of focusing on the higher aspects of inner being. Rather he claims all of life, moment by moment. He attends to everyday experiences, to sensory impressions, to descriptions of how he experiences his room, his activities, his body and its functions.

In examining one's own experiences and ways of reacting, a man comes to discover in himself a "master-form," a central pattern of individual personality. Montaigne provides in his own self-searching both a model and a guide for such exploration. He encourages other men toward the exciting individual truths to be discovered along the course of the intensely personal journey into the self.

However, he is also deeply interested in the universal insights one might come upon as to what in the self is simply most human. He is hopeful about such rewards because he believes that "every man bears the entire form of human nature."[13] Each man is trapped in his own biology, and the fabric of every man's life is partly woven out of the trivial, the everyday, the human.

In stressing this examination of one's own consciousness, Montaigne is not making a case for the contemplative over the active life. Rather he is stressing the need for each man to engage in some solitary reflection. Even in the midst of the most active life, a man must have the private thoughts that are prerequisite to independent judgment. A part of each man's self must be free of other's eyes. A part of each man's self must be all his own. This is no dour and bitter holding out on others, but a joyful celebration of one's own special self: "It is an absolute perfection and, as it were, divine for a man to know how to enjoy rightfully his own being. We seek other conditions because we do not understand the use of our own, and go out of ourselves because we do not know what it is like within."[14]

Montaigne showed great disdain for dogmatic systems that ruled out those parts of life that might contradict such theses. And he so valued that which was fundamentally human, that he loathed the authority that separated men, making them seem intrinsically different from one another. Yet in later years his own name was sometimes used to support an egocentric hyper-individuality, a position so self-centered and contemplative as to be totally apolitical; a humanism now devoid of concern for other men.

THE MAGUS

The Magus of the Renaissance was neither sorcerer nor magician. He was a seeker and a healer, who relied not on miracles nor on magic, whether black or white. He relied only on the hidden forces of nature, and like the intense Dr. Faustus, who was modeled after him, the Magus was tempted to sell his very soul to attain the secrets of the universe.

Such a man was the Magus, born Philippus Aurelius Theophrastus Bombast von Hohenheim, and known throughout Renaissance Europe as Paracelsus. This man was an itinerant, uncredentialled physician. It is not so much his work or even his teachings that serve as a metaphor for a psychotherapist, but rather how he viewed what was to be learned, how it was to be acquired, and how put into practice.

Most of his teachings are a conglomerate of theology, superstition, primitive (often fallacious) medical concepts, and somewhat righteous moralizing. Much of his work consisted of the independent study, teaching, and practice of medicine. But, too, he was also "astrologer, soothsayer, sorcerer, visionary, alchemist, maker of amulets and magic seals, etc., etc."[15]

What then can he offer us? He provides a new conception of the role of the healer. He sees God and nature meeting in man, and the practice of medicine as a priestly function mediating between God and the patient. Yet the physician remains his own man because "whenever God wishes to cure a patient, he does not work a miracle, but sends him a doctor."[16] In part, it is the efficacy of the physician's personality, his "healing word," that matters. The physician's concern is man's distress, both spiritual and material. The highest meaning of medicine is love.

Throughout his career, Paracelsus was at war with the authorities. He had the Renaissance distrust of absolute authority, but his defiance ran deeper than that. He believed that no one was too insignificant for him to be able to learn something from. Nor did he reject the acknowledged authorities out of hand. He even advised those who would be physicians to study every book on medicine that existed.

However, if a man is to learn, he must go out and observe things for himself. Established teachers are often more eager to hide their own errors than to fight their way through to the truth, more eager to protect their reputations than to put the needs of their patients above all else, at whatever personal cost. Therefore, the Magus advises others not to be upset by the fact that he is different in seeking out Nature as his teacher. He tells young aspiring physicians, "The patients are your textbook, the sickbed is your study."[17]

If a man is to learn, he must journey outward with eyes open to the world and inward with readiness to confront the reaches of his own soul. He counsels that "no man's master grows in his own home, nor has anyone found his teacher behind his stove."[18] He was, of course, resented, criticized, even persecuted by those who had already found the truth, made their reputations, and lost more patients' lives than they might have. But Paracelsus, the Magus, was too sure of himself to be appeasing or apologetic. The arrogance of belief in himself is made clear in his message to his critics and persecutors: "Even in the remotest corner there will be none of you on whom the dogs will not piss."[19]

What he did recommend to those who would teach was that they be those who practiced as well. A teacher must instruct with his hands as well as with his tongue. But not everything can be taught directly, and the student can only become a physician by learning "that which is unnamed, invisible, and immaterial, yet efficacious."[20] Partly, Paracelsus believed that there were some truths that would not be accepted, and some speakers of these truths might even be destroyed by the powerful and the ignorant.

However, his caution in this regard was not merely practical. In addition, he understood that some understandings cannot be reduced to simpleminded, concrete statements. Some truths must be stated in a way that requires that the listener bring something of his own to them if he is to understand. Paracelsus tells us (particularly he tells those of us who would guide others): "No magus . . . should tell . . . the naked truth. He should use images, allegories, figures, wondrous speech, or other hidden or roundabout ways."[21]

10 *Metaphors from Tales for Children*

A very young child is always at one with himself and a natural part of the world about him. He has many questions about the world: What is it called? How does it work? Who made it? But mostly he simply *lives* in the world, getting excited by it, tickled by it, bumped by it. He knows that he is the one who shouts or laughs or cries in response, who can do things or who cannot, who feels what others do to him and can make them feel some feelings, too.

So he lives in the world, and there is much about it that he does not understand, about which he is curious and/or scared. Yet he somehow never steps back to ask, "What's it all about?" He seems in a state of grace when it comes to matters of the spirit. Totally involved in living his life, he has neither time nor perspective in which to struggle with questions of identity or purpose or the meaning of it all.

Touch him softly and he will smile, hurt him and he will cry, catch his openness with some glittering, bouncy bauble of life and surely he will move forward easily and freely toward it. You can count on the young child to respond immediately in the here and now of his moment, but never will he stop to ask himself: "Who am I?" "What is the meaning of my life?" "How can I really be myself?" "What is my purpose in this crowded world?"

These questions do not begin to be asked until the child is an adolescent. That exciting, frightening, up/down time of transition from being a kid to becoming a grown-up is the time when spiritual questions arise. Lost is the innocence of childhood when you live in the world, simply a part of it, and it just seems that that's the way it is; when all you have to do is just be there.

All of a sudden, you are looking in on your life, and there is nothing so simple about it anymore. Grown-ups' answers may not at all be right, or may not be relevant to you in any case. "Let me look at myself," you say; "let me see how I feel. Let me try to understand so that I can live the kind of life that will make sense to me, that will make me feel best about who I am in the world, and about what my place is in it." Adolescence is a time to search for your own answers.

This spiritual seeking does not begin until adolescence. Perhaps that is why spiritual guides do not appear in tales for young children. Instead we usually find magic helpers who grant the wishes of the good characters and punish the naughty ones. Wish-granting and rescuing helpers (such as the Fairy Godmother in Cinderella and the Woodsman in Little Red Riding Hood) rarely require any self-understanding of the hero (with whom the child identifies).

Perhaps it is this very unselfconscious simplicity, so appropriate to the world of the young child, that is so boring to the dutiful adult who repeatedly reads or tells the tales to the child. I think of few exceptions, few tales with characters whom children like and yet whose problems touch familiar chords in the adult who is reading the story. It is only in children's tales such as these that the characters get into trouble because of the way in which they approach life rather than because some bad witch casts a spell on them. And it is only in children's tales such as these that we find a helper, healer, or guide who might serve as a metaphor for a psychotherapist. The two examples which we will examine are the *Winnie-the-Pooh* stories by A. A. Milne and the tale of *The Wizard of Oz* by L. Frank Baum.

THE WISE FRIEND

The Winnie-the-Pooh tales originated as stories made up by Alan Alexander Milne to please his little son Christopher Robin Milne. Christopher, himself, is the Wise Friend in the stories. The other characters are his very own stuffed animals, delightfully brought to life by his father's loving imagination.

Each of the characters has a very definite personality, typically one that embodies some common human foibles. The central character, Winnie-the-Pooh, is "a Bear of Very Little Brain," who does not think things out clearly. He avoids unpleasant realities for as long as he can. Instead he concentrates on whether it isn't "Time for a Little Something" (such as a lick of honey or condensed milk on some bread).

On the other hand, Eeyore, the Old Gray Donkey, spends too much time thinking about all the terrible things that might befall him. He tries to figure them out in advance and hardly ever has any fun. In his gloomy way, he is ever asking himself, "Why?" and "Wherefore?" and "Inasmuch as which?" He is so full of doubts that it sometimes seems to him that he has not felt anything else for a long, long time.

Rabbit is often imposed upon by all his "Friends and Relations" because he is too polite to say no. Tigger, the bouncy young tiger is just the opposite. He is destructively impatient in his search for personal satisfaction. In order "to find out what Tiggers like," he is forever bowling over the other characters in the stories. This aggressive behavior is especially hard on Piglet, who is afraid of almost everything. Of course, Piglet pretends that he is not upset, as when, "to show that he hadn't been frightened, he jumped up and down once or twice in an exercising sort of way."[1]

It is these very personality characteristics, these all-too-human hang-ups, that so often get these characters into trouble. And when in trouble, they usually turn for help to their Wise Friend, Christopher Robin. This wise friend is a boy who is patient, understanding, and loving. And what is more, Christopher Robin has a perspective that the others sadly lack. He is often the only one who looks at things as they are.

For instance, there was the time when Winnie-the-Pooh was wandering around, perhaps hoping to find a Little Something, when he came upon some paw marks. Pooh got Piglet to join him (so as to show that he wasn't frightened). Together they went round and round a large tree tracking what might "turn out to be Hostile Animals." Piglet came along because he was sure that instead it would turn out to be a harmless Woozle. But as this pair of mighty hunters circled the tree again and again, each time there were tracks of more and more Woozles. At last, they saw their Wise Friend, Christopher Robin, perched high up above them in the branches of a big oak tree. He came down to talk to them about their problem:

"Silly old Bear," he said, "what *were* you doing?" First you went round the . . . [tree] twice by yourself, and then Piglet ran after you and you went round again together, and then you were just going round a fourth time—"

"Wait a moment," said Winnie-the-Pooh, holding up his paw.

He sat down and thought, in the most thoughtful way he could think. Then he fitted his paw into one of the tracks . . . and then he scratched his nose twice and stood up.

"Yes," said Winnie-the-Pooh.

"I see now," said Winnie-the-Pooh.

"I have been Foolish and Deluded," said he, "and I am a Bear of No Brain at All."

"You're the Best Bear in All the World," said Christopher Robin soothingly.[2]

In this case, the Wise Friend's perspective and reassurance were enough. In other cases, this good counsel is only effective if the character who is in trouble is willing to pay the price for his foolishness.

Such another case occurred the time that Winnie-the-Pooh dropped in at Rabbit's hole unannounced, in hope of finding a Little Something. Rabbit was, of course, too polite to turn Pooh down. He was too polite even to stop Pooh when Pooh was eating every bit of honey, condensed milk, and bread in Rabbit's hole. At last, when there was nothing more to eat, Pooh attempted to leave. I say "attempted" because by now Pooh was so stuffed that he could only get halfway through the entrance to Rabbit's hole. And there, halfway through, Pooh was stuck until Christopher Robin, his Wise Friend, came along. It was clear that Pooh would have to remain stuck for a week before he would be thin enough to get free again.

"A week!" said Pooh gloomily. *"What about meals?"*

"I'm afraid no meals," said Christopher Robin, "because of getting thin quicker. But we *will* read to you."

Bear began to sigh, and then found he couldn't because he was so tightly stuck; and a tear rolled down his eye, as he said:

"Then would you read a Sustaining Book, such as would help and comfort a Wedged Bear in Great Tightness?"[3]

And, of course, Christopher Robin, did just exactly that for a whole week, as "Bear felt himself getting slenderer and slenderer." Some helpers feel that even if the person in trouble has to live out his own struggle in order to get out of that trouble, the helper can certainly offer something to sustain the troubled person throughout the ordeal. As we shall come to see, in the case of the Wonderful Wizard, some helpers do not feel this way at all.

THE WONDERFUL WIZARD

Therapist: I am Oz, the Great and Terrible. Who are you, and why do you seek me?

Patient: I am Dorothy, the Small and Meek. I have come to you for help. I am lost out here in this world, and I want you to get me back to Kansas, where I will be safe and comfortable.

Therapist: Why should I do this for you?

Patient: Because you are strong and I am weak, because you are a great Wizard and I am only a helpless little girl.

Therapist: But you were strong enough to kill the Wicked Witch of the East.

Patient: That just happened. I could not help it.

Therapist: Well, I will give you my answer. You have no right to expect me to send you back to Kansas unless you do something for me in return. In this country everyone must pay for everything he gets. If you wish me to use my magic power to send you home again, you must do something for me first. Help me and I will help you.

Patient: I will do anything you ask, anything. Only tell me. What must I do?

Therapist: Kill the Wicked Witch of the West.

Patient: No, that I cannot, will not do.

Most readers will recognize this bit of dialogue, as being more or less the way it appeared in *The Wonderful Wizard of Oz*,[4] although I have recast it as an initial exchange between therapist and patient. It was in 1900 that L. Frank Baum, self-appointed Royal Historian of Oz, published this first of his chronicles. He wrote it as the beginning of a series of modern wonder tales. But unlike the writers of earlier stories, he hoped to eliminate "all the horrible and blood-curdling incidents devised by their authors to point a fearsome moral to each tale."

Mr. Baum was writing, in part, as an expression of his own dissatisfaction with Victorian ideas of building character through punishment, grave lectures, and inner struggles for self-control, sacrifice, and self-denial. He visualized instead the possibility of personal growth through coming to accept ourselves, with humor if need be, and of the central role of a loving relationship in solving our problems. And, too, he believed that all of this could only be accomplished by our coming to learn that the powerful other, the authority, the Wizard to whom we look for help, is himself only another struggling human being.

The continued success of this book and of the motion picture made from it—their perpetually fresh capacity for reengaging us with delight in the adventures of their characters—is testimony to the compelling quality of his vision. In all of this I see some themes that are very much at the core of my own sort of psychotherapy. I would like, therefore, to reexamine some aspects of the wonderful *Wizard of Oz* as a psychotherapeutic tale.

In the original story, Dorothy, the little girl heroine of the tale, is an orphan who has come to live with foster parents, Aunt Em and Uncle Henry. Their home is dull and gray, as is everything else in the sunbaked, unyielding land of Kansas, U.S.A. Aunt Em is described as an unsmiling sober woman, thin and gaunt, who, when Dorothy first came, was so startled by the girl's laughter that it would cause her to scream and press her hand upon her heart. Uncle Henry is a man who never laughed, looked stern and solemn, and rarely spoke. It was only Dorothy's dog Toto and her good heart that made her laugh and saved her from growing as gray as her surroundings.

Early in the story, Dorothy is separated by a cyclone from her foster family and from the world of familiarly unhappy surroundings. The storm whisks her and Toto, together with their house, away from the plains of Kansas, U.S.A., off to the bewildering land of Oz. It is this crisis of being uprooted, flooded with fantasy, and no longer in touch with the familiar misery of home that leads Dorothy to seek the help of the Wizard of Oz in his great palace in Emerald City. Her house, it seems, had landed on the Wicked Witch of the East and killed her. Dorothy, of course, points out that this is in no way her fault. In fact, Aunt Em had told her that there were no witches living anyway. The Good Witch of the North (a good mother, at last) is of more help. She has Dorothy put on the Silver Shoes of the dead witch and refers her to the Wizard for treatment of her problems.

And so, like many patients, Dorothy seeks treatment, not out of having some perspective on her long unhappy family life, but rather in the midst of a crisis of the moment that separates her from her family or from her usual ways of handling things at home. It is so often not chronic unhappiness, but rather present confusion and situational distress that lead people to the office of the psychotherapist. All Dorothy wants is to go back home to the known safety of her unsatisfactory family life, rather than tolerate the promise of her new and unfamiliar world. *She prefers the security of misery to the misery of insecurity.*

On the way to Emerald City she meets other distressed creatures who need psychotherapy but do not know it is available until they meet Dorothy. They are, of course, the Scarecrow, the Tin Woodman, and the Cowardly Lion. The Scarecrow's problem is that he has no brains at all. Dorothy finds him perched on a stick in a cornfield, harassed by crows. He is the inadequate man, who acts foolishly and is sure that his foolishness is no fault of his own—he simply lacks what he needs to behave competently and wisely. In the meanwhile, people must not expect too much of him, but must protect him from fire because he is stuffed with straw.

Next Dorothy comes upon the Tin Woodman standing in the woods with uplifted ax in his hands, rusted so badly that he cannot move. His problem is that though he seems very polite, he has no heart. He once was a man of flesh and blood, but was hurt so often that he gradually had all the parts of his body replaced with tin. And, alas, the heart was left out. He, too, is not responsible for this unfortunate state of affairs. If only someone would do something for him, he might be able to really care about people instead of merely appearing to be polite. His problem with rust requires that other people be around to oil him up, or he just won't be able to function.

The third companion startles them in the woods. It is the Cowardly Lion, who menaces them with unwarranted mock ferocity but all too quickly reveals that he is nothing but a big coward. Although he has brains and heart and home, he lacks courage. Therefore, he cannot be expected to follow through with boldness, to risk himself, to act like a man—or rather like a lion. He roars to scare others off, but if they stay to challenge, he shows his cowardice. "But how can I help it?" he pleads and then tells Dorothy that, now that she knows this, she must be careful not to frighten him.

When all four know one another's problems, they set out for the therapist's office on a joint venture that you might expect to give them some sense of empathy and genuine consideration for one another. Instead, after their mutual disclosures, each mutters self-centeredly to himself.

The Scarecrow: "All the same, I shall ask for brains instead of a heart; for a fool would not know what to do with a heart if he had one."

The Tin Woodman: "I shall take the heart, for brains do not make one happy, and happiness is the best thing in the world."

The Cowardly Lion: "What they each want is certainly less important than courage."

And finally there was good sweet little Dorothy: if only she could get back home, she really wouldn't care whether or not the others got what they wanted.

Apparently the really important thing is to get one's own way.

When at last they arrive at the Palace in Emerald City, the Wizard does individual intake interviews with each of them. And as it is with new patients, each sees him very differently from the others. He appears variously to them as a lovely winged lady on a throne, an enormous head, a ball of fire, and a most terrible monster. Each approaches him as Dorothy did: "I am Dorothy, the Small and Meek.

I have come to you for help . . ." Each is frightened and helpless, and somehow this entitles each one of them to special help and consideration, which the Wizard absolutely must give, simply because he is adequate and strong. The Wizard, good therapist that he is, quickly comes across as a person who has his own needs. In therapy country, everyone must pay for everything he gets. That means these poor helpless patients must give something of themselves if they wish to get something for themselves.

The task which the Wizard assigns is that they must kill the Wicked Witch of the West. They would like the Wizard to destroy the bad mother for them, but no matter how great and powerful a father he seems to them, he cannot do for them what they must do for themselves. He cannot even tell them how to go about it. Each patient tries to "cop out" in his own way. Dorothy has already "accidentally" killed the Wicked Witch of the East, but this time she must kill willingly and not by accident or without responsibility. She is reluctant because she cannot be forceful on purpose. Scarecrow says he will not be able to help because he is a fool; Tin Woodman because he does not have the heart for it; and Cowardly Lion because he is too fearful. In order to help them, however, the Wizard will not let them off the hook.

So, reluctantly, they set off to slay the Wicked Witch of the West. In the course of this adventure, in spite of themselves, they become caught up with being a part of it and with genuine concern for one another—so much so, that the Scarecrow makes wise decisions, the Tin Woodman acts out of loyalty, and the Cowardly Lion performs bravely. Eventually even Dorothy is able to be happy for her friends and their achievements, even when she fears she may never achieve her own desires.

This task assigned by the Wizard is a kind of teaching by indirection. As in psychotherapy, he insists that they will get nowhere if they simply continue to bewail their fates and to stubbornly insist that because they have troubles, he must magically solve their problems (or at least be terribly sympathetic). Instead he directs their attention elsewhere.

In individual therapy we may get the patient to focus on his past history. In group therapy, we may encourage the patient's curiosity about the group process. Some of what occurs as the patient reluctantly takes on these tasks is that he can begin to lose himself in the sense of giving himself over to the assigned work. As this unhooks him from his willful, self-sorry demand for someone to give him relief right now, a new possibility arises! The patient can now begin to experience the therapist and the other patients as real people with selves of their own; as people who have meaning outside of himself, who can therefore be meaningful to him, and who can ultimately put him in touch with the meaning of his own life.

Once our adventurers have accomplished what they first insisted they could not possibly do—that is, the slaying of the Witch—they return to the Wizard, impatient for their rewards. They have not yet realized that they already possess them. In the course of asserting themselves at the Wizard's palace, they reveal to themselves that he is not a Wizard at all—he is "just a common man," or worse, a humbug! When he is challenged, it turns out that he has problems of his own. Disillusioned, Dorothy tells him, "I think you are a very bad man." "Oh, no, my dear," he answers, "I'm really a very good man, though I'm a very bad Wizard, I must admit."

The Wizard then tries to help them to understand the solutions at which they have already arrived. For the Scarecrow, it was not a problem of lacking brains, but of avoiding the experiences that would yield knowledge. Now that he would risk being wrong, he could sometimes act wisely. So too with the Tin Woodman: it was not a heart he lacked, but rather a willingness to bear unhappiness. And, of course, the Cowardly Lion needed, not courage, but the confidence to know that he could face danger even when he was terribly afraid. Then Mr. Baum, with sympathetic tolerance for human foibles, has each patient still insist that the Wizard confirm his accomplishment with some external token. In one version, the Wizard presents the Scarecrow with a Diploma, gives the Tin Woodman a Solid Gold Watch for Loyal Service, and awards the Lion a Medal for Bravery.

As for Dorothy herself, she learns that all this time all she had to do to get home was to use the Silver Shoes she has had on. She needs only knock the heels together three times and the shoes will carry her wherever she wishes to go. That is, she has learned that she has the power to go wherever she wants to go and to make changes in her life if only she is willing to take the responsibility of recognizing and using that power.

Of course, the Wizard could have told them all this at the beginning of treatment, but they never would have believed him. How could they have accepted that they were demanding from others simple human qualities that they already possessed? The insights are too simple to be grasped, too obvious to see, and can only be had when a person stops demanding them from the powerful Wizard/Parent who is supposed to take care of him. He must give up the struggle with himself and become involved with another, and with what can be between them.

Mr. Baum revitalizes old lessons which must be learned again and again: acquiring wisdom involves risking being wrong or foolish; being loving and tender requires a willingness to bear unhappiness; courage is the confidence to face danger, though afraid; gaining freedom and power requires only a willingness to recognize their existence and to face their consequences. We can find ourselves only when we are willing to risk losing ourselves to another, to the moment, to a quest, *and love is the bridge.*

But last of all, alas, there are no Wizards! And yet, as a psychotherapist, I am sometimes tempted to join the Wonderful Wizard of Oz in saying, "But how can I help being a humbug, when all these people make me do things that everybody knows can't be done?"

11   *Metaphors from Science Fiction*

Among science fiction enthusiasts, there is a saying: "Science fiction of today, Science of tomorrow." Space travel is perhaps the most dramatic instance of such dreams come true. But the projections of science fiction writers have not been restricted to plausible extensions of science and technology. In some instances, the science fiction tale involves an attempt to help us to see where we might be headed in other terms. Not only the tools and weapons of contemporary man, but also his attitudes and his social institutions may yet lead him toward heaven or into the depths of hell. In some of the science fiction writings we can discover projections of future helpers, healers, and guides, as well as prefigures of their deadly counterparts. One such sinister guru is the Director of Hatcheries and Conditioning.

THE DIRECTOR OF HATCHERIES AND CONDITIONING

Every utopia has its price. Is it ever less than exorbitant? This question is examined by Aldous Huxley in his science fiction classic, *Brave New World.* Written in 1932, this novel was an attempt to serve an early, and as yet unheeded, warning. Earlier than most, Huxley, even then, was aware of some of the dangers of twentieth-century man's thrust toward a mushrooming technology, unevenly distributed fruits of overproduction, and gluttonous consumption of luxuries.

He realized that Western man had come to grasp at the promise of Science as the yearned-for panacea, as the possibility of turning civilization into a latter-day Eden. Of course, for this society to realize its fullest technological expansion rapidly enough for those who were already somewhat comfortable to be able to enjoy its fruits, those who were traditionally less comfortable might have to endure some further hardships. But then that's the only way *they* know how to live.

Indeed, everyone might have to endure certain individual sacrifices for the good of mankind. In the long run, it would certainly be best for everyone if Science and the State could somehow merge into a benevolent technocracy. The necessary enlightened controls would be built into the system. Individual rights would be less of an issue. People could be helped to do what was best for them (and for everyone else). At last, all could know the coming of a brave new world, a utopia born of man's technological know-how, serving everyone's needs as it would be decided they should best be served.

The brave new world is a time and place in which spiritual problems are solved in advance, by the grace of governmental planning and control in the form of scientific programming and prevention. The new guru, the helper, healer, and guide of the new world, is the technocratic state personified by the Director of Hatcheries and Conditioning—the D.H.C. The agency which the D.H.C. directs is the major instrument of social stability on a planet whose one-world motto has become: "Community, Identity, Stability."

The predestining and conditioning of infants begins before birth, though the D.H.C. complains that "you can't really do any useful conditioning till the fetuses have lost their tails." In this new scientific era, of course, the embryos no longer need to develop in the uterus. Instead, they are grown in specialized scientific equipment at the Hatchery. In that way, their chemical environment can be varied so that babies can be "decanted," already predestined for one of the social castes (designated as Alpha, Beta, Gamma, etc.).

Each baby is at birth (or when "decanted") already ideally suited biologically for his social role (ranging as it might from moronic servant to sensitive aristocrat). It only remains then for the D.H.C. to condition the baby to be psychologically suited for his role in life. To accomplish this, the D.H.C. has the caste-segregated infant nurseries set up as Neo-Pavlovian Conditioning Rooms.

For example, in a Delta infant nursery, khaki-clad infants are being prepared for being satisfied with simple mechanical work. Flowers and colorful books are put out on the floor for them. These infants of eight months crawl eagerly toward them. The D.H.C. gives a signal, and the head nurse pulls down a little lever. Suddenly, the quiet gives way to shrill sirens and loud alarm bells. The children scream in terror. Now the D.H.C. signals for the electrified grid in the floor to be turned on, shocking the children into pain and panic, "to rub in the lesson."

No more will these Delta children approach books and flowers. No books will mean no ideas to make them discontent with their mechanical lot. No flowers will mean avoiding the economic problems of the past when such masses flocked to the country. These children will grow up to stay in the city and consume all of the manufactured items they must to support the State's economy. Consumption of goods is the mainstay of this technocracy. If something seems worn, throw it away, for "ending is better than mending." This and other slogans constitute the heart of the moral education of the people of this brave new world. These homilies are taught by tape recordings played while the children sleep. This sleep-teaching, or hypnopaedia, instills all that is needed, from basic slogans like "Everyone belongs to everyone else" to the specific teachings about caste and consumption.

The needs and desires of people are manipulated and turned toward those goals which the State finds it most useful to offer, useful in terms of its own self-perpetuation. Frustration is held down to a minimum so that no one is "compelled to live through a long time-interval between the consciousness of a desire and its fulfillment."[1] Any moment of dissatisfaction which slips through the network of programmed "happiness" is obliterated by *soma*, the perfect drug. It is "euphoric, narcotic, pleasantly hallucinant," and government-sponsored. Soma has "all the advantages of Christianity and alcohol" without any of their defects. If the D.H.C.'s work has not solved all problems for all time, a dose of soma provides a holiday from reality whenever needed. Remember, "One cubic centimetre cures ten gloomy sentiments."[2]

THE MINISTER OF LOVE

Huxley's Director of Hatcheries and Conditioning has the job of programming each child for his life as a happy consumer. He preconditions each of his wards to fit into that role that will serve best to perpetuate progress in the technological society. In the process, the D.H.C. sets up each citizen's needs so that this brave new world can fulfill them without needless frustration. The price of this state of contentment is the loss of individual freedom and self-determination.

George Orwell's later science fiction novel, *Nineteen Eighty-four*, is another utopian nightmare. Huxley warned of the dangers into which the idealizing of Science may lead us. Orwell tells us that we must beware of giving the State a great deal of power in the misguided hope that it will take good care of us. He extends in fantasy that which he sees as the already inherent totalitarian menace. The danger arises when those who run the government try to control the thinking of a citizenry whom they insist do not know what is good for them.

Winston, Orwell's hero, lives in the year 1984 in the midst of such frightening benevolence. Everywhere there are enormous posters of the Leader's face, with eyes that seem to follow you about when you move. The caption on each poster reads:

BIG BROTHER IS WATCHING YOU

There is no escape. Even at home, there is a compulsory telescreen, a sort of "improved" TV which transmits propaganda and watches the viewer at the same time. It cannot be completely shut off.

Winston himself is one of the fortunate elite, a Party member, who participates in the running of things. He works in the Ministry of Truth, that part of the government which controls news, education, entertainment, and fine arts. His job in the Records Department is the rewriting of past speeches and news releases. This "reconstruction of the past" allows the State to deal with new developments without running the risk of ever being wrong.

For instance, one day there is a news release telling of great military victories, and as usual it is followed by a demand for greater sacrifices. In this case, the individual chocolate ration is reduced from thirty to twenty grams per week. A few days later, another news release tells of "spontaneous demonstrations" which have taken place to thank Big Brother for *raising* the chocolate ration to twenty grams per week. Soon afterward Winston is instructed to rewrite one of Big Brother's earlier speeches so that he will have appeared to have predicted this raising of the chocolate ration.

Despite Winston's favored position, he is still subject to telescreen scrutiny and must participate in the compulsory, scheduled ritual vilifications of "enemies of the State" during Hate Week. Physical training is required so that he maintain the stamina to serve, and he must maintain the same appearance of willing acceptance of this as of all his other obligations to the State. The watchful eyes and ears of the Thought Police (and of patriotic citizens) make it necessary for him to watch what he says lest he be prosecuted for a thoughtcrime. Even his facial expressions may be monitored, so that a grimace occurring at a time when a smile is demanded may result in prosecution for a facecrime. He knows that at any time he can be "vaporized." If this happens, not only will the Thought Police have dragged him off into the night, but if it is advantageous to the State, all record of his existence on earth will have been expunged along with his disappearance.

Nonetheless, Winston has a residual inclination to think for himself, supported by the awareness of contradictions that is provided by his position with the Records Department. The catalyst in this unstable mixture is the woman Julia. Though she wears the traditional narrow scarlet waist sash, this emblem of the Junior Anti-Sex League is belied by Julia's enthusiastic commitment to eroticism. The State has long been involved in eradicating the sexual urge, along with all the other pleasures which might compete with the desire to serve. Thus, Winston and Julia's lovemaking itself is an act of political defiance.

Winston becomes increasingly committed to political freedom. No longer will he accept the Party slogans:

WAR IS PEACE

FREEDOM IS SLAVERY

IGNORANCE IS STRENGTH

He is now puzzled by the Doublethink, which had previously allowed him to believe that a thing could be both true and untrue depending on how it related to the State. He goes so far as to remember and talk about what had gone on in the past, before it was reconstructed.

At last his political disaffection comes to the attention of the Thought Police, and he ends up deep in the cellars of the Ministry of Love. In 1984 it no longer seems unlikely that the branch of government that maintains law and order is a windowless, barricaded, well-guarded, steel-doored fortress, a dreaded place called the Ministry of Love. In this totalitarian age, the healer of the soul has become a sadistic agent of the State, risen to a position of refined cruelty—the Minister of Love.

Winston's encounter with O'Brien, the Minister of Love, consists of his being tortured, for his own good. Winston has been mad enough to question the dictates of Big Brother, and now O'Brien must "cure" him. The first part of the cure involves conditioning his thinking with electrically-induced controlled pain. The Minister of Love tells Winston:

You know perfectly well what is the matter with you. You have known it for years though you have fought against the knowledge. You are mentally deranged. You suffer from a defective memory. You are unable to remember real events, and you persuade yourself that you remember other events which never happened. Fortunately, it is curable. . . .[3]

In order to "cure" Winston, the Minister of Love must be able to change his thinking, his perception, his memory. The emphasis on memory is crucial. This is made clear in the Party slogan:

WHO CONTROLS THE PAST CONTROLS THE FUTURE
WHO CONTROLS THE PRESENT CONTROLS THE PAST

Memories which do not fit with the State's reconstruction of history
are "delusions." Experiences which do not concur are "hallucinations."

The Minister of Love is not interested in merely changing Winston's
behavior. He seeks the abject submission necessary to leaving nothing
but Winston's sorrow for what he has done and renewed love for
Big Brother. Confession and punishment are not the goals. They both
know that everything else follows if the freedom is granted to say
that two plus two make four. O'Brien knows that Winston must
undergo "an act of self-destruction," that he must "humble himself"
before he can become sane. And so the Minister of Love subjects
him to a scientifically systematic program of torture aimed at getting
him to "see" five fingers when only four are held up, because the
Party says there are five.

Finally, after many nightmarish days, Winston has "been kicked
and flogged and insulted . . . screamed with pain [and] rolled on
the floor in . . . [his] own blood and vomit."[4] Still, he has not been
sufficiently degraded. The Minister of Love warns; "We shall squeeze
you empty and then we shall fill you with ourselves."[5]

Only one final degradation is needed—that he betray Julia, not
only in his words but in his very heart.

In order to accomplish this, the Minister of Love must resort to
the final step, Room 101. Room 101 contains "the worst thing in
the world." For each citizen its contents are different. For Winston,
Room 101 contains rats. He cannot even think about rats without
being terrified. Now he is faced with a cage from which rats will
be released to attack his face. He finds himself screaming, "Do it
to Julia! Not me."

He has been completely cured by the Minister of Love. He is
thoroughly penitent and filled with gratitude toward Big Brother for
redeeming him. In his joy and renewal, he can no longer remember
that while he was still mad, the Minister of Love had told him, "If
you want a picture of the future, imagine a boot stamping on a human
face—forever."[6]

THE PLANETARY EXPLORATION AND SETTLEMENT BOARD

Not all science fiction predicts so nightmarish a future. Some tales
describe a tomorrow full of promise, while others merely explore

the possibilities with a seemingly neutral curiosity. In Robert Sheckley's story "The Minimum Man," the hero is an inadequate fellow who would be a completely recognizable figure in our own time. In Sheckley's world of the future, he receives therapy by accident, as an unforeseen outgrowth of the exploration of space. A Planetary Exploration and Settlement Board serves as the planner of the therapeutic milieu, and Robot serves as an alter ego.

We find our hero, Anton Percerveral, at the age of 34 about to commit suicide. He is forever screwing up. No accident or minor illness evades him. Whatever is small enough to misplace, he loses. Larger things he manages to break. Job after job is lost, and satisfying friendships are impossible to come by. He has undergone Analysis, Hypnotic Suggestion, Hypnotic Hypersuggestion, and Countersuggestion Removal. No form of treatment was beyond the impact of his inadequacy.

His suicide attempt is similarly unsuccessful. It is interrupted by a telegram from the Planetary Exploration and Settlement Board. He is offered a job as an Extraterrestrial Explorer, a job for which he had earlier been turned down. He protests to the Planetary Board that this must be an error. Haskell, the representative of the Planetary Board, explains that in the early days they chose only the most competent men as explorers, men who could survive anywhere that human survival was possible. But now that overpopulation created so great a demand for colonization of land in which the most ordinary men could survive, the qualifications for explorers had changed. Now, instead of using optimal-survival explorers, they sought minimum-survival men, men such as Anton Percerveral. Such men are contacted when their hopes have run out, when suicide seems imminent.

Anton, seeing that the job is no more dangerous than suicide, decides to take the Planetary Board up on its offer. He is sent to the unexplored planet of Theta, with a Robot as an assistant. Soon enough he finds that much of his equipment either malfunctions, breaks, or wears out. He contacts Haskell, only to learn that these failures are control elements for maintaining minimal survival conditions.

Anton reacts to all these built-in foul-ups (which for once in his life are not of his making) by learning to repair, take care of, and properly use all of his equipment. However, his newly developing survival talents are counteracted by the growing destructiveness of the Robot. He learns from Haskell that the Robot is a flexible quality control for maintaining the minimal survival conditions. As Anton becomes more skillful and less accident-prone, the Robot's behavior deteriorates. As time goes on, Anton

learned how to live with the Robot. . . . The Robot now seemed the embodi-
ment of that other, darker side of himself, the inept and accident-prone
Percerveral. . . . The Robot came to represent his own destructive urges cut
loose from the life impulse and allowed to run rampant. Percerveral worked,
and his neurosis stalked behind him, eternally destructive, yet—in the manner of neurosis—protective of itself.[7]

With the help of some of the mole-like inhabitants of Theta, Anton
buries the Robot underground and then spends his own time improv-
ing his survival skills. At last he feels not only that he himself has
become adequate, but that he is ready to declare Theta safe for the
survival of other ordinary men. In the name of the Planetary Board,
Haskell warns that the Robot, that personification of Anton's neurosis,
may have been only temporarily set aside and not yet fully destroyed.

Haskell is right. With the aid of self-repair units, the Robot reap-
pears, more destructive than ever. Anton prepares a series of traps
for the Robot, but none of them work, for

how can a man trick the trickiest part of himself? The right hand always
finds out what the left hand is doing, and the cleverest of devices never
fools the supreme fooler for long.[8]

At last Anton realizes that he is going about this in the wrong way.
He sees that "the way to freedom is not through deception." He must
give up trying to conquer the Robot, and concentrate on overcoming
his kinship with it. When it is no longer *his* neurosis, but simply
a neurosis, it will lose it power over him.

Filled with new confidence, with enthusiasm, with laughter, Anton
simply trusts himself and moves with whatever feels right within
himself. The clumsy Robot is thrown by its own weight, and Anton
is free at last. His work is done. Haskell arrives on Theta as a representative of the Planetary Board, coming on the colony ship *Cuchulain*.

Haskell tells Anton he has been successful. The planet is ready
for colonization, and he may remain there for the many rewards he
is to receive. Anton wants to go on to explore some other planet,
but Haskell points out that he no longer qualifies as a minimum-
survival person. Anton turns away in disappointment, stumbles, spills
some ink, trips, and bangs his head. But Haskell is not to be fooled.
Anton must live up to his newfound adequacy.

In this story, scientific developments for curing neurosis are men-
tioned, but they all fail when applied to Anton. Successful therapy
comes to Anton in the form of the Planetary Board, those who encourage exploration and risk-taking. The Planetary Board sets the scene

but is unconcerned with Anton's getting better. The Planetary Board arranges that Anton must face the destructive forces in himself (in the form of the Robot), not just bury them.

In this story, the Machine represents the neurosis. In Bradbury's "The Lost City of Mars," the Machine is the therapist.

THE MACHINE

Ray Bradbury writes about a chronically unhappy married couple wandering through an aging, abandoned city on the red planet of Mars. These people, who trudge along the empty streets past the cracked windows of empty shops, are the poet Harpwell and his wife Megeen.

They are battling as they always do. He is calculatingly obscene, and she is dependably righteous and condemning. She sums up her complaints about him, "The whole thing is . . . you only came along so you could lay hands on the nearest woman and spray her ears with bad breath and worse poetry."[9] To all of this, he can only answer, "Ah, God, I've curdled inside. Shut up, woman . . .," and lapse into more obscenity. The interplanetary Harpwells are a latter-day Dylan and Caitlin Thomas.

At last, the poet runs off in a rage, escaping into an abandoned building, the doors of which slam and lock behind him. Within the building, Harpwell finds himself in a great domed room which houses a large, complicated Machine with a sort of a driver's seat, complete with steering wheel, dials, and switches. Never able to leave anything dangerous alone, the poet seats himself at the wheel, flips a switch, and grabs tightly onto the steering wheel as the great Machine seems to shiver, bolt, and dash ahead.

Suddenly he finds himself in a car, racing down a highway at ninety miles an hour. Coming toward him at the same deadly speed is another car, maneuvering reciprocally to obviate his every attempt to avoid a head-on collision. There was no brake, no stopping the crash. There was only his scream, the terrible collision, the tearing apart of metal, the explosion, and the broken torch it all became. Harpwell lay dead, but only for a while.

He found himself not only alive again and once more seated at the controls of the Machine, but, what was more, he found himself interested, fascinated, indeed, exhilarated. For a moment he thought of Megeen and wished she were there to see it all, but only for a moment. Again he flipped switches and tinkered with dials, seeking another "diversion." This time it was the cars all over again, only much faster. Again the crash, the dying, the reviving only to feel even more alive. It was "queer beyond queerness."

Again and again, he dialed and switched on the violence, the dying, and the reviving. Faster and faster, he set the pace. Eventually, for the cars, he substituted locomotives approaching on the same track, ramming jets, missiles screaming through space toward each other.

Bit by bit he began to see what the Machine was all about:

I begin to know what this is used for; for such as me, the poor wandering idiots of the world, confused and sore put upon by mothers as soon as dropped from wombs, insulted with Christian guilt, and gone mad from the need of destruction and collecting a pittance of hurt here and scar tissue there, and a larger portable wife grievance. . . . We do want to die, we want to be killed, and here's the very thing for it, in convenient quick pay! So pay it out, machine, dole it out. . . .[10]

Half an hour later, he is sitting at the Machine, beginning to laugh. He is happy in a way so new and so promising that he need never drink again. He has been so really hurt and punished enough at last that he need never be involved in another self-destructive act for the rest of his life. His guilt has been paid for. His need to be destroyed has been finally satisfied.

Happy at last, and grateful too, he finds his way out of the building. Outside is Megeen, ready as always to begin the screaming once more. But the poet is free at last, "off the Christian hook." No longer needing the mental punishment of life with Megeen, he wanders off laughing joyously. Bewildered, his abandoned wife wanders into the building which houses the Machine. Sniffing and scowling, she is seeking some new opponent. The doors close behind her.

12 *Metaphors from the "Now Scene"*

THE PSYCHEDELIC GUIDE

Ours is a drug age. There is no longer any need to face pain and uncertainty. If you're young enough, you can smoke grass. If you're old enough to fear that marijuana will make you a dope fiend, you can sit around and discuss the drug problem over well-chilled extra-dry martinis. Or as one matronly suburban housewife decried, "I'm just sure that my daughter is using drugs. This morning, when I went to the medicine cabinet, I discovered that some of my tranquilizers were missing."

Of course, life-softening chemicals have been used for centuries, particularly in Asia and the Middle East. Roots and herbs having the power to provide pleasure have long been valued, given ritual meaning, and used lovingly. But in the burgeoning technology of the present, it has become possible to produce synthetics and chemicals that quickly come into wide use. There does not seem to be time for their producers to test out the dangers in laboratories, nor patience for their users to examine whatever evidence of their effects is available.

The drugs, which are most used by the young in our culture, range widely from the seemingly harmless gifts of pleasure, such as marijuana and hashish, to the deadly killer drugs, such as heroin and "speed" (amphetamines). There is, however, a strange middle ground of powerful hallucinogenic or psychedelic drugs such as "acid," peyote, and "magic mushrooms."

These psychedelic, mind-changing, or consciousness-expanding drugs are both old and new, natural and synthetic. "Acid" (LSD-25) is a recent discovery, a laboratory product first synthesized in Switzerland in 1938. Peyote, in contrast, is found in the buttons of certain cactus plants which grow in the American Southwest; it has been used in certain Indian religious ceremonies for centuries, and in recent years it has been synthesized in a form called mescaline. Similarly, "magic mushrooms" have long been considered sacred producers of ecstasy by the Indians of Mexico, and their effects, too, are now available in the form of a laboratory-produced synthetic known as psilocybin.

There are differences in the effects produced by taking different psychedelic drugs. Nonetheless, whatever the differences, those who encourage the use of psychedelic drugs claim that there is one central effect common to them all: any psychedelic drug can result in the manifesting of unexplored areas of the subject's mind. His consciousness will be expanded to include previously unknown parameters of his own being and of his place in the universe. He will experience a "trip," a journey into himself, into his own mind and perhaps into the universal consciousness.

This is a journey that can be dangerous to make alone. It is too easy to have a bad trip, a "bummer." The subject can become "uptight" and "paranoid," caught in a seemingly endless nightmare, a crazily terrifying experience. It is sometimes said that a bad trip is not so much a matter of actually running into something terrible within oneself, as it is a terror-stricken flight from whatever it is that one *might* encounter in the unplumbed depths of one's mind.

Who will accompany the subject on this frightening, exciting journey over unfamiliar terrain? Who will lead and assist him in the exploration of his altered, expanding consciousness? This is the task of the Psychedelic Guide, who will conduct the subject safely and rewardingly through his drug experience. To do this, the Psychedelic Guide needs to have had some extended experience in taking mind-manifesting drugs himself. He must understand the psychological changes through which a man may go, be able to cope with psychological crises, and be able to "manipulate the subject . . . without . . . dominating" him.[1] The medium for his influence is an atmosphere of trust, which he must be able to create in the subject.

The Psychedelic Guide's work may begin before the actual drug-taking session. He meets with the subject in advance, sometimes in several pre-drug sessions, during which he prepares the subject by giving information, clearing away misconceptions, and establishing rapport. During the drug session, the Psychedelic Guide helps the subject not to lose his way. Subsequently, he sees the subject for post-drug sessions to answer questions and to see that all is going well.

For the drug session itself, the Psychedelic Guide provides a pleasant human setting. The drab, antiseptic, authoritarian qualities of clinical settings are too often experienced as alien and menacing by the subject who is tripping. It is often enhancing to the subject's exploration of his drug experience to provide provocative sensory stimuli such as interesting music, paintings, and sculpture, as well as interesting objects to smell and touch such as flowers and fruits.

The subject may begin his trip with a particular goal in mind, such as the seeking of a mystical experience or the attempt to solve an unyielding interpersonal problem. While such wishes are to be honored, the Psychedelic Guide must help the subject to take the experience as it comes and to follow it wherever it may lead. He must facilitate the subject's explorations while keeping his own influence at a minimum.

The first stage of the Psychedelic Guide's task within the actual drug session involves guiding the subject through new experiences in the sensory realm. He may place various pictures and objects before the subject and encourage him to "enter into friendly or harmonious relationship" with these vegetables and flowers, these stones and seashells.[2]

This heightened sensory awareness is a world of its own and often results in continued sensitivity to beauty long after the drug session. Sometimes it can lead directly to the second stage, during which the Psychedelic Guide can help the subject to begin to explore some personal problems. For example, taken with the delicacy of a flower petal, the subject may turn toward the unexplored delicacy of some of his feelings toward other people. Through this exploration of personal problems, the Psychedelic Guide must support the subject's feelings of trust, encourage him toward positive feelings, and interrupt his getting rutted in despair and self-criticism.

It is often helpful at this stage if the Psychedelic Guide has, in the pre-drug sessions, tuned in on some of the key words or concepts around which the subject's life pivots. When this is done successfully, the subject may experience the guide as telepathic as they simultaneously grasp subtle, hidden, or multiple meanings of what is going on. Here is an example of an illuminating experience in which both the Psychedelic Guide and the subject are open to the meanings of a psychedelic pun:

SUBJECT: (*to Guide*) You smile.
G: The earth smiles.
S: (*Accepts a stone G hands him and examines it.*) The smile in the heart of the matter. But does it matter? Does anything . . . matter?
G: Go into the stone and find out.

S: (*Studies the stone for several seconds and speaks without taking his eyes away from it.*) Yes, I matter . . . Deeply, I matter . . . In the very heart of creation I . . . matter.
G: And your "nothingness" that you were complaining about a while ago? Where is it now?
S: (*Looking up and weeping tears of joy*) When Being begins, Nothing matters.[3]

The openness of the Psychedelic Guide to the breadth and depth of the subject's experience can be greatly enhanced if the guide himself has a widely diverse background that includes "knowledge of history, literature, philosophy, mythology, art, and religion."[4] This is of particular importance in the third or symbolic stage of the trip. It is here that the subject's experience is likely to be represented in symbolic images, born of the world of legend and myth. If he understands, the Psychedelic Guide can help the subject to feel a sense of his own place in the process of history and in the evolution of his species.

Some few subjects seem to be open to a guide's accompanying them to an even deeper level of integration. Here the subject experiences a merging with the mystical stream, a profoundly transforming experience, which gives him a new sense of his place in the universe. This may be experienced as a confrontation with God, with the Ground of Being, or with some Fundamental Reality. It has the rewards (and the limitations) of a religious conversion for the subject, and often of a shared religious experience with the Psychedelic Guide.

THE EX-ADDICT

There are those who praise psychedelic drugs and those who condemn them, those who see them as the hope of mankind and those who see them as the seeds of his downfall. But when it comes to the use of heroin, no one seems to be in favor except the self-deluding beginning user who is in the process of getting "strung-out" or addicted, and the parasitic pusher who makes his living out of the misery of the junkies whom he supplies.

The junkie may start out using heroin when he is looking for thrills, trying to avoid unhappiness and uncertainty, or merely trying to maintain his status among his peers. However, if he uses heroin often enough, he will end up seeking it because his body craves it, because it is the one sure way to feel good (at least briefly). He will need more and more, spend most of his waking time wondering where he can get more and how he can pay for it. Eventually, he will be ready to lie, cheat, steal, sometimes even kill, to get what he wants.

He may want out of this cycle of degradation and destruction, but if he wasn't dishonest to begin with, by now he will certainly lack the courage to face what he must do and to stick to it. His world is a world of lies and excuses. He cannot bear to be without the heroin he needs. Whatever promises to do otherwise he may make will be broken. The best of therapists do not seem to be able to work successfully with him. How can he be helped to break free from his excuses? Perhaps he can only be gotten through what he must do with the help of someone who has gone through it himself. Perhaps only the Ex-Addict can help the using addict.

The most important aspect of having an Ex-Addict treat another addict is that he knows all the excuses, no longer uses them to protect himself, and is unlikely to be fooled when someone else tries to use them. The heroin addiction itself is a fairly cut-and-dried issue: "Getting the white heroin powder through theft or prostitution; cooking it up with water in a bent, dirty spoon; drawing the concoction up through a needle inserted into an eyedropper; and injecting it into a 'live' vein tells almost the complete, absurd story of the symptom drug addiction."[5]

Confronting the addict when he tries to explain away his habit is quite another sort of issue. It takes not only the personal knowledge which permits seeing through an addict's cover story, but the courage to confront him on it. The straight talk begins when the addict arrives at the communal living setting in which he will be helped by other Ex-Addicts. From the outset, he is referred to as "a using dope fiend." He is told that he is stupid to destroy his life as he has. If he wants the respect of the other house members and of the older Ex-Addicts, he must gradually demonstrate his capacity for honesty, courage, concern for others, and willingness to take on responsibility.

In small group encounters, he is confronted again and again, first about personal gripes others may have against him, and increasingly about the patterns of irresponsibility which emerge in his behavior. These might include playing out the role of being a mamma's boy, a tough guy, or a lazy slob. He will be given verbal "haircuts" by the older Ex-Addict and other group members, called out into the open in what may seem like a brutal form of attack therapy but one that leaves him nowhere to hide out. The first time he tries to spin out some long rationalization for his behavior, some elaborate psychological explanation, the group will encourage him until he is way, way out on a limb, which the Ex-Addict will then saw off by

shouting, " 'You lying son-of-a-bitch, you're so full of shit, it's ridiculous.' With that everyone in the group . . . [breaks] up in a loud
roar of laughter."[6]

To live in the Ex-Addict community, the addict must observe two
basic restrictions: no drugs, alcohol, or chemicals; and no violence
or threats of violence. Within these limits the Ex-Addict can help
the "dope fiend" to face himself, to learn to take responsibility for
himself, and to find the supportive sense of community that will allow
him to withstand the pressures that tempt him to turn once more
toward heroin and away from life.

THE ENCOUNTER GROUP LEADER

In his work with small confrontational groups, the Ex-Addict may
be viewed as a specialized example of a broader category of new
gurus on the contemporary scene, the Encounter Group Leader.

Encounter groups are new. Encounter groups are now.[7] You may
hear them called T-groups, lab groups, or more formally, training
laboratories in group dynamics. Such groups may also be referred
to as sensitivity training groups, basic encounter groups, or workshops
in human relationships.

Encounter group sessions may last a few hours or run from one
day right into the next. Sessions may be repeated for a couple of
days or may extend over a period of several weeks. These meetings
take place in many parts of the world, usually in retreats or personal
growth centers, but also in educational, religious, and correctional
institutions, in private offices and in homes. Participants include not
only drug addicts, but also students, teachers, businessmen, parishioners, and mixed groups of experience-hungry adults and adoles-
cents. Individual groups usually consist of from eight to eighteen
participants.

These differences among encounter groups matter far less than the
goals they share and the common ways in which they attempt to
reach them. All encounter groups are *intensive group experiences that
focus on each person's awareness of himself and his relationships with other
people.*

The responsibility of the Encounter Group Leader is to facilitate
the expression of thoughts and feelings by the group members. He
must help to make it *their* group. One of the ways this is accomplished
is through the Encounter Group Leader setting for the group the task
of observing and responding to what goes on in the group session.

They are urged and helped to stay in the present rather than to depend on past events and old conceptions. The focus is always on the *here and now* rather than on the *there and then*.

The group members will be inclined to demand that the Encounter Group Leader tell them what to do. He may then begin by focusing their attention on the ways in which they depend on his direction rather than discovering for themselves where they are and where they want to go. In addition to reflecting feelings and focusing attention, the Encounter Group Leader may also encourage participation in non-verbal activities. Learning about yourself and other people by silently touching one another and asserting the presence of your own body by letting it do new and unexpected movements are the sorts of activities the Encounter Group Leader may facilitate to provide "experiences of great intensity and considerable personal change."

The Encounter Group Leader's facilitation may rest squarely on his own personal participation, on his willingness to risk something new and unexplored in the here and now of the group. As one Leader puts it:

I am convinced that the attitude of the facilitator has a very profound influence. If he trusts, people tend to be trustworthy. If he mistrusts and for whatever reasons manipulates, people tend to become distracted from the quest of finding their own sources of inner direction.[8] If . . . I am able to pay close attention to what feels right to me and risk being myself, I have found that this, in turn, allows others to accept and be themselves.[9]

As the group facilitator, the Encounter Group Leader provides innovation, personal presence, emphasis on freedom rather than structure, and the offering of support without manipulation. All of these combine to allow people to learn to become aware of and to value their own feelings, to become part of a group without losing their own individual identities, and to remain themselves in a group without violating the feelings of others.

The intensity of the experience for each group member and the profound impact it may have on his life-style attitudes are hard to imagine, given so brief an encounter. They are vividly reflected in one participant's response to the other group members who not long before had been total strangers! "I would have gladly given my life for any person in that room."[10]

We might wonder, why this need for intense personal interaction, for touching, for being known? In part, this desperate search can only be understood in the context of the failure of twentieth-century man's success.

THE STRANGER

Twentieth-century man has developed technology that supports him in ways too complex for him to understand. He depends on computerized planning, which works so long as each man is an interchangeable unit. He lives in communities so large and impersonal that he is anonymous and alone. Abstracted from the immediacy of his own life and so often out of touch with others, he is dead to his own feelings except for a sense of nameless anxiety, anguish without object.

Religion seems irrelevant. Science, once a promise, is now a threat. Academic philosophy has no answers. In Plato's time, philosophy was a passionate pursuit. Now it has become a matter of so many words, devoid of meaning. Empty categories and complex analyses cannot be felt as a concern for human existence. At this point, partly as a response to Europe's despair over two devastating world wars, a new way of reaching into life arises. Existential Philosophy is felt as a new, strange, exciting presence. At the center of Existential Philosophy is "the individual human personality itself struggling for self-realization."[11] Out of this comes a new dimension in psychotherapy, a confrontation of Stranger to Stranger, trying to get to know one another.

A person whom I do not yet know is appropriately called a "Stranger," that is, he who is strange to me, even as I am to him. When we are both confronted with the possibility or the necessity of personally engaging one another in a newly forming relationship, each of us is faced to some extent with the anxiety with which all men respond to the unfamiliar or the unknown. To the degree that I can live in the present and feel strong enough to face challenges and to tolerate uncertainty and ambiguity, I am able to offset the anxiety I bring to the situation by a sense of pleasant excitement and an anticipation of something new and promising. If this be the case, I can override or set aside my fears and really listen to the other, so as to allow him to emerge into the light as a person in his own right, new and fearsome though this may be. Corresponding possibilities exist in him as well.

On the other hand, to some extent each of us still lives in the darkness of his own unfinished past, trying to hide from the chronic fears about who he might really turn out to be. To the extent to which this is true of me, the other person will remain a Stranger whose true being is hidden and who is seen only in the distorted image cast by the shadows of my own unhappy past. The inauthentic quality of our encounter would be further compounded by whatever distortions he brings to our meeting.

These distortions may also occur in any of the momentary sizing-up maneuvers used by comparatively open individuals as they temporarily forestall coming to grips with a new person. In an attempt to call forth the admiration of the Stranger, such a person may, for instance, begin a conversation by presenting his credentials with some introductory statement of his own prestigeful origins, social position, status job, or artistic-intellectual interests. Or, in contrast to this, he may be self-demurring, apologetic, or terribly interested in the accomplishments of the other, in order to please the Stranger and to put him into a receptive mood. The socially prescribed small talk about the weather and the like maintains a more neutral atmosphere in initial encounters, but at the same time offers even less of a chance for Strangers to come to understand one another.

In each of these as well as the many other "how to meet new people" devices, we try to maintain an image of ourselves that we find comfortable, while seeking out the cues that we use to fit new people into stereotyped images out of the past. For example, how often when we are to meet someone new do we ask, "What does he do?" rather than "Who is he?" In light of all this, it sometimes seems amazing that we ever do genuinely get to know each other at all. Nonetheless, most of us do seem to need some such devices as opening gambits with which to put the Stranger and ourselves at ease as we brave the first encounter.

Unfortunately, to the extent that any one of us is emotionally disturbed, such gambits constitute a way of life rather than a momentary holding action. In this sense, what has been called "mental illness" may be viewed as an ironic caricature of the general human condition. Throughout all of their relationships, some of those called neurotics cast themselves in roles such as attacker of the unjust; others as the helper of the weak, unfortunate among the lucky ones, admirer of the strong, or helpless one among those upon whom he must depend. There is a seemingly endless number of varieties of such neurotic role-takings. Yet they all appear to have one quality in common: in order to preserve their own pseudo-identities, these people must get others to take on the reciprocal roles, to play the evil stepsister to their Cinderella, the Dragon to their Saint George, or Desdemona to their Othello. This may be accomplished through threat, flattery, or pathetic appeal.

It takes a psychotic individual to seem to be able to totally disregard the reality of others' social behavior in favor of his own delusional expectancies. Yet even the most confused behavior of the schizophrenic appears to have its own unconsciously sought-after impact on those around him. For the less disturbed person, however, it is only possible to maintain the character defenses of these social roles by securing the reciprocal supporting response of the people with whom he plays this desperate game. When others no longer reciprocate (because he goes too far or offers too little), the neurotic is forced back upon the more classical, less social expressions of unhappiness (such as the obsession or compulsion).

All of these various character defenses are ways of maintaining the status quo, ways of remaining a Stranger to the Stranger. The neurotic avoids options that imply new experiences, thus escaping from any genuine encounter with another human being. This avoids any revealing of the mystery of another's personality and, in the process, protects him from risking living out any new aspects of himself. By avoiding the risks implied in authentic living, he never loses except by default; but so too, he can never win. Rather, he sits out the game of life.

These problems, like so many others that are common to all men at one time or another, are the daily fare of the neurotic. And so, though they are the concern of all men, they are of special importance in psychotherapy.

From the beginning, the patient tries to keep the therapist a Stranger. He treats the therapist as an object, a theatrical prop, which he would cast in a role that fulfills his old familiar fantasies, his simultaneous fear and wish to say what his parents were like. Most important, he does not wish to know the therapist as a person. Only as a Stranger can the therapist fill his expectations.

In a general way, because of the therapist's self-chosen role of professional helper, an attempt will be made to use him as a source of relief or as a dumping ground for the wearisome burden of personal responsibility for the patient's own despair. However, in so dehumanizing the therapist, the patient gives up his own humanity. This very deterrent to any authentic interaction does, however, lay the groundwork for therapy insofar as the disturbed patient is always *himself*. I mean this in the sense that he uses the same defensive gambits within the session as he does in the world.

Let us assume that the therapist is a relatively mature human being, comfortable with his knowledge of who he is and ready to find out what others are really like. He comes as a Stranger, ready to be known, to meet another Stranger whom he would like to come to know.

Still, he is faced with his own problems in response to the patient. To begin with, he is in the paradoxical position of being paid to take on an attitude of genuine caring for a Stranger. His job then is to be concerned with and to help a person who comes to him for aid, but who asks for it in a way aimed at avoiding any genuine interaction. Furthermore, the therapist must avoid the temptation to use the patient as a way of justifying his being paid and feeling adequate (i.e., by pushing himself to do something for the patient). The patient, in doing his best to remain a Stranger to this Stranger and to avoid any real changes, creates some feelings of helplessness in the therapist. In response, the therapist may then be tempted to take cover behind his own characteristic ways of remaining a Stranger.

The therapist must see that the patient's defensive operations are not yet directed toward him as a person. He may not wish to put up with what *is* directed toward him, but it is helpful to see that the patient may be dumping feelings onto the therapist without ever having found out what sort of person the Stranger really is. He must be open to caring about the patient's unhappiness without feeling an obligation to rectify his misery. He must not try to do for the patient what the patient must do for himself.

If the therapist is indeed free of such problems, how then does he counter the patient's dehumanizing attitudes? At times, he may be tempted to reinstate his own sense of self at least momentarily by treating the patient as an object rather than as a person whom he might come to know. All therapists find that this happens from time to time, and the wise ones learn something from such errors, something about themselves and about their patients.

Somehow the therapist must counter the patient's onslaught by maintaining his own personhood in the face of it. He must continue to be willing to be known, to show who he is. He must be able to bypass the patient's defensively willful maneuvers by continuing to treat the patient as a person in his own right. The patient remains someone whom he wants to come to know in spite of all of this. The patient is entitled to his own feelings, but he is not necessarily entitled to the response which he demands from the therapist.

The therapist comes as a Stranger, but one who is willing to be known. His own struggle to be open and to be genuine may then offer hope to the patient. He may come to learn that his freedom consists in having the courage to recognize its existence. He must choose his freedom, knowing that each man is free to do as he pleases if only he agrees to face the consequences of his acts. Only then can he give up being a Stranger to another Stranger. Only then can he dare to know himself and to come to know another. And we had best do this, for in this world we have only ourselves and each other. It may not be much, but that's all there is.

III   *The Coming to Pass*

13 The Inevitability of Failure

"The oak is felled in the acorn . . ."

—DYLAN THOMAS

Nothing lasts. Everything that lives, dies. The note of doom is concealed in each moment, from the very first. Dylan Thomas has not so much a tragic view of life as a deep, long look into the very nature of things. He sees "the boys of summer [already] in their ruin".[1]

The dying begins at the moment of birth. Life is a journey. The traveling may be different for each man, but the destination for each man is the same. No matter who you are, "like a running grave, time tracks you down."[2] Birthdays are mileposts, as when Dylan describes a time as "my thirtieth year to heaven."[3]

This is no plot against man. It is just the way it is. Without death, there is no life. Without destruction, there is no creation. Without decay there is no growth. Whatever the force that gives, it is the same one that takes. "The force that through the green fuse drives the flower . . . is my destroyer."[4]

Whatever a man may do to distract himself, to try to forget that he must die, to set himself seemingly apart from the biological context, the process goes on: "A process in the weather of the heart/Turns damp to dry. . . ."[5] He may give himself to the joy and celebration of the lusty life. He may be "tickled by the rub of love" and yet not free: "And what's the rub? Death's feather on the nerve?"[6]

What is a man to do? First, he must let himself know not only of the inevitability of his ultimate passing, but of the decay going on at this very moment. There is change going on which he cannot change, for he himself is a part of it. Dylan tells us in terms so disgustingly scatological that we cannot forget them when he says: "I smelt the maggot in my stool."[7] He will not look away. He will not fool himself. He will not live through the fraudulent vision that does not see what it does not want to see. Instead, he will "sit and watch the worm beneath my nail wearing the quick away."[8]

But make no mistake. This is not a man without hope. Rather, it is a man who says there is no hope without eyes open to the dread. It is in knowing he must die that a man may live. The human spirit has meaning only as it knows the chains from which it is freed. Only in the willingness to know that we live only for a moment, that we are helpless and afraid—only in this knowing can we find something more. Only if we forgo certainty can we know. Only if we give up control can we determine where we go. Camus tells us that it is necessary "to learn to live and to die, and in order to be a man, to refuse to be a god."[9]

And Dylan, for all his feeling of being trapped in the inevitable decay of growing, in the inescapable end that exists in every beginning, is not without hope. He knows that "death shall have no dominion."[10] If a man can face his death and is still willing to live, if he knows he must be destroyed and yet will love, then "Though lovers be lost love shall not."[11]

It is necessary that a man give himself wholly to his life, even unto his dying. There is a lusty, raucous way to go, and yet there is a quietness and tenderness to the going as well. A man must die, but not until his death. He must not give up, must not surrender to the dying. He must burn out rather than be snuffed out. And so it is that Dylan tells his own dying father: "Do not go gentle into that good night./Rage, rage against the dying of the light."[12]

Dylan sings of this vision of "deaths and entrances,"[13] of no beginnings without endings. Not only does he see the autumnal dryness in the warm, wet green of spring, but too, he knows that in the stillness the song is born. He sees "the pulse of summer in the ice"[14] He knows that though the living die, Life goes on. But he sings for one man at a time, and each man's dying is his own, though Death be everyone's. Though he must die, a man must risk all, do what he must, and live till he dies. He should "not fear the apple nor the flood."[15]

Dylan's vision for each man, can be a vision for all men. That is, the processes of growth and decay in each individual man are mirrored in the evolvement and decline in the activities of the communities of men. Social processes are born, grow, deteriorate, and disappear, all only to be born again.

Progress is an illusion! All that is human is ephemeral. Everything we build begins and ends in a day. Even the Great Pyramid, whose long day cost so many lives, shall know the dust of its twilight. The Pharaoh for whom it was built has created a monument to his own arrogance, no more. And that too shall pass.

So it is with man's attempts to solve the problems of human sufferings as well. Each solution breeds new problems. In technical matters, we solve the problem of excessive infant deaths only to find that we have contributed to further population explosion and to adult deaths by starvation. It seems that Evil can be displaced, but that it can never be eradicated.

Even the growth of spiritual leadership is not spared. It too will rise only to fall once more. Nothing is accomplished once and for all. Sometimes it seems to me that anything worth the doing will need to be done again and again so long as human beings survive. Some of the best efforts of man arise in response to dealing with his own worst failures. Yet in each new success is the seed of new failures. And perhaps, the greater the capacity for good in any new venture, the greater the promise of substantial evil in its eventual corruption and decline.

The corruption of gurus is, of course, more complex than my description up to now might suggest. Any given spiritual leader may become corrupted. The sort of guidance and leadership that he provides may fall into decline. His disciples may fall short of the standards that he originally set. And any and all of these changes may occur in many ways and for many different reasons.

The nature of the decay that I have cited for a particular guru and the causes that I have ascribed to his decline are simplifications of complex social, psychological, political, even economic processes. In each case, I have chosen and discussed a form of corruption that seems most clearly associated with the guru to whom it is ascribed. Yet, in no instance do I mean the listing of the deteriorative process to be taken as a sufficient explanation for the disappearance, the arrest, or the transfiguration of the particular kind of leadership that is being described. In no case do I mean to suggest that such subtle social interactions occur in a single mode or for a single cause. I hope that my examples of corruption will stand as instructive highlights without seeming to be misleadingly comprehensive.

Perhaps most of the modes and causes of decline that I have cited occur in the corruption of most gurus, only patterned differently, with given processes being crucial in certain instances and peripheral in others. My attempt has been to insist that we face the impending decay of anything we value lest we ignore and so unwittingly hasten the disintegration we would deny. I wish to point here, and here, and again here, without ever meaning to say this is it, this is the one, this is all and there is no other.

The very life seems to drain out of even the most exciting spiritual movements, and the most electrifying of spiritual leaders may become ploddingly oppressive. Often a charismatic leader arises in a revolutionary context, standing over against a traditional or bureaucratic structure that is stifling the spirit of the people. And yet, after a while there is an ironic transformation, which Weber calls the *"routinization of charisma."*[16] The ultimate values that initially inspired the followers of the charismatic leader, the concerns that fired them to do what they must at any price, too soon give way to practical considerations, questions of expediency.

Once committed to individual inspiration of the moment, to flexibility and spontaneity, the gurus too soon begin to institutionalize their own accomplishments. They take their own efforts too seriously and gradually turn their organizations into the very sort of oppressive social institutions that they arose to overthrow. The very inspirations or techniques that they once used to make men free now themselves become idolized into forces of oppression. Unwilling to allow the continued risking of uncertainties that once projected them into the position of spiritual leadership, these gurus forgo their charismatic gifts for more reliable, orderly, self-perpetuating ways.

The inspirational ways that once stood them in good stead, that touched and moved and freed the spirits of their followers, become deadened by the very efforts to perpetuate them. Involvement gets sidetracked into concern with methodology. There is the temptation to feel that what has once been helpful must go on, without realizing that it may be helpful no longer. In order to preserve the good for the future, the guru becomes infatuated with the past. He will not let die what must die if new things are to grow. He makes "the error of treating one dead self not as a stepping-stone but as a pedestal."[17]

This cycle of alternate freeing and imprisoning of the human spirit by the all too human gurus is clearly exemplified in Judaism. The Teachers of the Torah began their efforts as an insistence that the singularity of their students not be lost before the majesty of the Law. Eventually their Talmudism ossified into a tradition-bound rationalism of its own, an empty legalism within which the entrapped Torah study had little room for freeing the individual spirit.

The Masters of the Kabbala rose up against this entrapment to seek, and to lead others toward, the ecstasies of the mystical experience. The routinization of their charisma came in the form of an increasing commitment to elaborate methodology. They lost any real personal contact with their students. Soon they were more like magical authorities who alone had access to the great Truths. Their followers had to come for favors in awe and humble supplication, rather than for the spiritual joys in which the earlier Masters of the Kabbala had once invited them to participate.

Hasidism arose, in part, in answer to this oppression, to offer a new mysticism, a personal and relevant spiritual adventure. For a time, the new gurus, the Zaddiks, freed their followers from the deadening influence of the dying institutionalized Kabbalism. But, in its own turn, the revolutionary fervor of the Zaddiks dissipated, giving way to petty bureaucratic concerns and a new, oppressive paternalism.

Changing attitudes of the followers of the guru also contribute to the routinization of charisma, to the institutionalization of spiritual leadership. Sometimes "the original doctrines are democratized. they are intellectually adjusted to the needs of that stratum which becomes the primary carrier of the leader's message."[18] So it was with those who followed the gurus of Taoism in the Orient. The more popular the Way became, the more it degenerated. The people found it difficult to remain open to the passive letting-go that Taoism inspires. They were more at ease with positive programs, clear methodologies, and certain goals. Thus it was that the subtly provocative, elusively freeing vision of the Masters of the Tao was reduced by their followers to superstition, health cults, alchemy, and magic.

The followers of Confucius brought a comparable decline. His disciples had at first been engaged by their Teacher of Ethics in an open dialogue about practical situations. He had taught that certain aspects of conduct were mere conventions. Understanding this, guidelines could be discovered that would facilitate living in peace and harmony. His disciples, in quest of certainty and perfection, codified this understanding into an elaborate set of rules of conduct that the superior man must master.

Thus the unwillingness of the followers to leave the guru's message fluid and flexible can result in their analyzing the magic away, routinizing the inspirational qualities, and idealizing the life out of his leadership by codifying it into a set of perfection-seeking rules.

Another variation on this problem of the disciples' debasing of the guru's freeing spiritual influence is the issue of the unenlightened converts. Among the followers of any particular guru, there will be some who are enlightened by a kind of direct and transfiguring illumination. As in the case of any religious conversion experience, the person feels turned around by what he has gone through. He feels transformed and sees the world and his own life in a wholly new light.

But there are always other disciples whose "conversion" is less convincing. These followers are changed by the "Second-best expedient of a kind of social drill,"[19] or imitation, which allows them to "perform mechanically" what they might not have been able to come by on their own initiative. So long as the guru is present to enliven and direct their unwitting parodies of his teachings, there is no disaster. In fact, the followers are usually unaware until his leaving that his teachings are separate from his person. But once the guru is gone, the life may go out of his teachings. So it was with many of the disciples of the Compassionate Buddha, whose teachings became hollow once he was gone. Parroting what he had taught brought none of the depth of meaning that his personal presence had inspired.

Men, briefly inspired, are doomed to become "rational" once more. Sometimes it's a simple matter of economics. With the evolution of an agricultural economy, the fiery Shaman of the hunting and gathering societies gave way to the sensibly orthodox Priest. Charismatic leadership gave way to traditionalism; imaginatively individual guidance and inspiration yielded to "enduring institutions and material interests."[20] Camus has pointed out that today's revolutionary must become tomorrow's heretic if he is not to become tomorrow's oppressor.[21] Every post-revolutionary reign of terror teaches this, and yet we never seem to be able to learn.

Spiritual leadership may be corrupted by becoming like the oppressive institutions against which it arose, or paradoxically, it may fail by becoming an overstated caricature of itself. The human qualities and involvements that can be most creative are also the ones that can be most destructive. Sexual longing, anger, pride, the craving for power—these weaknesses/strengths of man are daimonic, as in "any natural function which has the power to take over the whole person."[22] As gurus, both the Apollonian Oracle and the Dionysian Mad God became exaggerated extensions of what they started out to be, grotesque caricatures of their own initially creative thrust.

The Oracle, Apollo, who began as the spokesman of reason, of order, and of form, searching for balance and for harmony, ended up as a rigid enforcer of inhibition and repression, demanding perfectionistic self-control and the extinction of human passions. The Mad God of the Cult of Dionysus, who at first inspired celebration of the senses, ecstatic abandon, and the joy of creativity, later provoked an insatiable seeking of the most grotesque depravity, a frantic lusting after new thrills for the decadent.

Another danger to spiritual leadership is the idolization of the person of guru. Toynbee points out that a major nemesis to creativity of social groups, one that may arrest their growth, lead to their breakdown and eventual disappearance, is the "idolization of the ephemeral self"[23] of the group's leader. This can occur when the guru gradually comes to be seen by himself and by his followers as being elevated above all other men. His teachings and the followers for whom they were intended become depreciated as the guru is deified.

The apotheosis of the Zaddiks came about when their Hasidic followers elevated them above all other men and when the Zaddiks themselves were tempted by this opportunity for sainthood. So, too, the heartbreakingly gentle devotion of the fourth-century hermit monks, the Spiritual Fathers of the Desert, could not long withstand the so human temptation to arrogance. Their instruction to their disciples, which began as attempts to turn the younger brothers away from petty prideful concerns, to help them to submit to their spiritual selves, more and more became unreasonable, domineering demands for blind obedience and self-degradation.

This profoundly human situation of being trapped in the cycle of humble devotion and arrogant disservice has been touchingly portrayed in Agee's description of the spiritual struggle of a twelve-year-old Catholic boy, a boy who might be any of us. It was in the early dark of Good Friday morning that the boy, Richard, was awakened to begin his Easter vigil, the morning watch during which he was not to desert sweet Jesus alone on the Cross.

Richard struggled to resist one worldly distraction after another. In the past, he had not really given himself to being with Our Lord but had instead thought of other things, waiting for the time to pass, had resented and even cursed having to be in the chapel at all. But this time it would be different. This time he really believed. He loved Jesus and would be with Him. He thought of nothing else. His knees hurt cruelly and his back ached and ached as he remained closely attentive to his prolonged, prayerful kneeling. He let himself understand how Christ must have suffered, imagining so vividly what it must be like to be crucified that at that moment "he felt a tearing spasm of anguish in the center of each palm and with an instant dazzling of amazed delight, remembering pictures of great saints, shouted within himself, *I've got the Wounds!*"[24]

Immediately he realized that what he had done was both blasphemous and absurd, that he must confess to this ridiculous bit of pride, even though it grew out of his wish to give himself completely to Jesus. But even as he became contrite, tried once more to face his humiliation, and determined to make a clean breast of it in Confession, it occurred to Richard that

not many people would even know this for the terrible sin it was, or would feel a contrition so deep, or would have the courage truly and fully, in all of its awful shamefulness, to confess it; and again the strength and the self-esteem fell from him and he was aghast in the knowledge that still again in this pride and complacency he had sinned and must still again confess; and again that in recognizing this newest sin as swiftly as it arose, and in repenting it and determining to confess it as well, he had in a sense balanced the offense and restored his well-being and his self-esteem and again in that there was evil, and again in the repenting of it there was good and evil as well, until it began to seem as if he were tempted into eternal wrong by rightness itself or even the mere desire for rightness and as if he were trapped between them, good and evil. . . .[25]

Perhaps, then, there can be no escape from the perpetual rising and falling of the spirit of man. Perhaps the greatest danger lies in bringing about the corruption more quickly and more completely than need be by our not facing our helplessness before the inevitability of its coming. Perhaps we can only be free if we do not try to escape our imperfections, if we see that we can only be what we wish to be, from time to time, and only briefly at each time. Perhaps, we must go on forgiving ourselves again and again, forever.

14 The Third Force

"Though they go mad they shall be sane."

—DYLAN THOMAS

The struggle continues today. The search still goes on for a more viable kind of personal help for the troubled. Psychotherapy is the twentieth-century attempt to achieve the improved, the ultimate, the finally lasting form of spiritual guidance. The three major conceits of modern therapy have been Psychoanalysis, Behavior Therapy, and the "Third Force" of Humanistic Psychology.

Each in its own way has been successful in helping troubled people. But only one thing seems sure: that none of these faces of the new guru will turn out to be an eternal visage. Each approach is useful, each is creative, and each turns out to be ephemeral. Each approach is but a temporary misconception in the history of man's quest for the illusion of stability and certainty in a life that is ever-changing and fundamentally ambiguous.

As I approach the maelstrom of forces set in motion and countermotion by the gurus of my own time, I become aware of how much simpler it has been for me to be open to accepting the offerings and the limitations of the gurus of other times and places. Here, today, in my own world, I experience the turmoil of my passionate personal commitments and angry disaffections. It is so very tempting to fool myself into choosing between the good guys and the bad guys, to pose as the free spirit of dissent against the oppressive Establishment, to despair over the past and to hope for too much from the future. In their own times, the Hasidim, the Desert Fathers, and the Taoists must certainly have experienced such compelling self-deceptions. Who am I that I should not suffer the same temptations?

PSYCHOANALYSIS

Psychoanalysis was conceived by Sigmund Freud near the end of the last century. As with the other forms of guruship, of spiritual guidance, it arose in a revolutionary context. Psychoanalysis tore away

131

the stifling blanket of Victorian prudery to reveal man as an instinc-
tual, sexual being. Further, this new way of understanding went
against the physical-mechanical methods of nineteenth-century
science, reopening the "scientific" study of man to the more speculative traditions that at that time had been reserved for philosophy
and religion. The Freudian Revolution was more comprehensive than
most that we have considered so far, delivering as it did the third
hammerblow of science to the already battered arrogance of modern
man.

The first blow was heliocentrism. Man had thought himself the
center of the universe until Copernicus came to tell him that the
trivial sphere on which he lived was but one of several orbiting its
mother Sun. Perhaps the heliocentric man was not so special in the
universe, but at least he could assure himself that he was set apart
from the animal kingdom here on Earth. He was a wondrous creation
like none other. Then came Darwin with his Theory of Evolution.
His bad news was that man's own ancestry was no different than
that of other beasts, that he was not a separate and elevated sort
of being.

This left early twentieth-century man having to define his special
place on earth in terms of his unique inner resources. Of all the
beasts, only he knew what he was doing. Only he had Reason. Then
came Freud with "the Unconscious" as his "god-term," teaching us
that we only *seemed* to act in reasonable terms, that really we acted
out of old, hidden, irrational motives. Not only were we largely unaware of these driving inner forces, but, he showed us, we could
be shocked and appalled to learn the nature of them.

Psychoanalysis was not only "a method of medical treatment for
those suffering from nervous disorders,"[1] but a new way of viewing
man, a radical philosophical outlook. Because of this, the first generation of psychoanalysts included many freethinking mavericks, men
who felt stifled by the world view within which they had grown up,
men willing to risk all on a commitment to a new, exciting, revolutionary approach to human suffering. What a lesser breed are those
of their inheritors who run Institutes of Psychoanalysis from which
a candidate can be certified only if he emerges with orthodoxy in
his mouth and lead in his heart.

Psychoanalysis is not, of course, a system sprung full-grown from
the forehead of Freud at a particular moment in history. Freud's own
ideas changed and developed over the years, and he has generously
exposed and shared the struggle and the excitement of this metamor-
phosis in his writings. Many of his disciples took issue with both

his theory and his method (some at the cost of his friendship). Some neo-Freudians and other advocates of change revised Psychoanalysis, for example, by reconceptualizing the Freudian sexual drive as the central motive force, replacing it with the seeking of power (Adler), with an undifferentiated universal life urge (Jung), or with the search for interpersonal security (Horney and Sullivan). The development of these and other variations took courage and imagination and are certainly worth studying in their own terms.

Yet I am treating Psychoanalysis here as though it were a more unified approach. This is not because I believe that the variations were meaningless, but because Psychoanalysis no longer fascinates me and because in so brief an excursion I prefer to emphasize those aspects which I believe are central to the method.

Too, I do believe that it is nonsense to change and change and change an approach, and still to insist on calling it by its original name. As some psychoanalytic positions have grown and evolved, strongly influenced by newer nonpsychoanalytic ideas and practices, the psychoanalytic gurus have been guilty of an insidious form of academic imperialism. Each exciting development gets labeled "a new advance in Psychoanalysis." It's a bit like the modern technological superstates (such as the U.S. and the U.S.S.R.), which, as Marcuse[2] has pointed out, are able to perpetuate themselves by absorbing, diluting, and claiming as their own, any form of dissent that challenges their dominance or threatens their overthrow. What cannot be incorporated is vilified and debunked, as in "America's" present comic/tragic rejection of so many of its most imaginative youths as "hippie-commie-fags," and as in cultist psychoanalytic reduction of criticism to neurotic "resistance" (a defense against facing unacceptable truths from one's unconscious).

Nonetheless, Psychoanalysis has been monumentally helpful to some troubled people. It has also been fertile ground for the growth of new outlooks on perennial problems, culminating in "the emergence of the psychological man,"[3] replacing earlier conceptions of man—the pagan political man, the Christian religious man, and the Enlightenment's economic man.

What then did Psychoanalysis teach that could so fundamentally influence man's view of himself in the world? First of all, Psychoanalysis taught that every act of man had a cause and, therefore, that all of his behavior could be understood. Even errors, jokes, and slips of the tongue could reveal underlying meanings and motives. Dreams, which had earlier been discarded as nonsense or, at best, understood only in magical or superstitiously prophetic terms, became important scientific data. Indeed the interpretation of dreams was "the royal road to the unconscious," because "when the work of interpretation has been completed, the dream can be recognized as a wish-fulfillment."[4]

These unsuspected wishes are often the unfulfilled longings of childhood. Freud has shown us that far from being angelic and innocent, each little child is motivated by powerful sexual and destructive urges, torn by the ambivalence of loving and hating at the same time. Too weak to have his way and made anxious by the threat of punishment, loss, or oblivion, he "represses" his incestuous, homicidal, and cannibalistic wishes. Not only are these wishes actively forgotten, buried in his unconscious, but anything that reminds him of his anxieties about them is also avoided. He may develop a reasonable conscience as a protective concession to the parental retaliative authority that he fears, still leaving himself much room for a full life and surreptitious expression of his secret urges. An example of this compromise of seeming both to give in and to have one's way might involve displacing onto someone else those feelings originally directed toward a parent (such as rebelling against the authority of a boss because of anger toward a father). Another way of making-do is sublimation, in which the grown-up finds a symbolic expression of the forbidden childhood urge, which is then acted out in a disguised, socially acceptable form (such as a woman becoming a nurse, and thus secretly replacing the mother).

Given too much frustration of wishes or too little support of the needed ways to hide or transform these wishes, a person may grow up to be a neurotic, filled with anxieties and fixated or stuck at some infantile level of dealing with the world. If he comes to a Psychoanalyst, a careful history of his childhood will be taken. Then he will be assigned to lie on a couch and instructed in the method of free association. In this way he is to learn to say whatever comes to mind, without censoring or editing, no matter how silly, trivial, crazy, or offensive his thoughts might be. With the aid of the psychoanalytic guru's infrequent interpretations of what his associations "really" mean, he can be led back to the childhood memories of the original psychic struggles and so make conscious and manageable what was formerly poorly repressed (unremembered and yet disruptive).

But this is not sufficient. For these insights to be truly transforming and freeing, they must be experienced emotionally. This takes place within the medium of the relationship between the analyst and the patient. The psychoanalytic guru sits out of sight of the patient, rarely speaks, reveals as little as possible of himself as a person, and avoids any personal or social interactions with his patient. The patient develops strong feelings of love and hate, of longing and dread, which are interpreted as "nothing but" the transference of childhood wishes and fears. The romance and tragedy of the nursery is now transferred from the parents of old onto the blank screen presented by the analyst. The analyst may even experience the countertransference of his own unresolved infantile fragments (which he must work out for himself or resolve by reconsulting his own analyst). The patient's feelings and wishes must be exposed for the infantile fantasies they represent, and analyzed away so that he may become free of his fixations. The mutual regard and trusted closeness of guru and disciple, so valued in the past, is now viewed as merely an instrumental phase of the psychoanalytic process. The charisma of the guru is "no longer a personal gift . . . but a technical function."[5]

Other lively aspects of the original excitement of discovery have also been reduced into the dully deadening remnants of a self-perpetuating, closed system. The writings to be found in psychoanalytic journals presume to analyze, not only clinical situations, but politics, art, and religion as well. In the end, all is reduced to "nothing but" a sublimation, or a rationalization, a projection, or an introjection of some long-repressed infantile struggle. Continued exposure to this material so inundates the reader with predictable sorting into preconceived categories that he finds it is less like studying a conceptual analysis than like reading a tightly contrived literary style which can turn *Hamlet*, the Russian Revolution, and the Roman Catholic Church into intricate elaborations of the allegedly universal Oedipus complex.

Earlier, Freud was a revolutionary, come to emancipate the Victorian world from the oppression of prudery. It is in part his success that has contributed to the growing sexual permissiveness of our age. Now we may be headed for the other edge of the abyss, the loneliness born of empty impersonal screwing, rather than of hidden, shameful lust. But what is to be the role of the psychoanalytic guru in the post-psychoanalytic world? "If, as it may appear, Freud and the movement of which he is a part have already largely accomplished their emancipative task, from what now can Freud liberate us?"[6]

BEHAVIOR THERAPY

The Psychoanalysts have always been fascinated with imaginings about those inner processes that make man most human: his wishes, his fears, his dreams. They are moved by men's struggles. They wish to heal his emotional ills by journeying into the depths of his psyche. True, what they cannot heal they elaborately explain away in terms of the patient's "not being ready for analysis," his having been "spoiled for analysis" by prior nonanalytic treatment, his "resistance" to the treatment. Explanation takes the place of evaluation and self-criticism. Still, they have helped many, given us an excitingly new view of man, and have been committed to learning "the secrets of the heart."[7]

Toward the end of the 1950s, a new guru emerged, the Behavior Therapist, who defined himself as a critic of these speculative romantics. Behavior Therapy was initiated, not by clinicians (let alone, by spiritual leaders), but by laboratory scientists. Their intent was to evaluate objectively the effects of different kinds of treatment, to bring to bear the findings of detached scientific efforts, and to transform therapy from a search for deep insights into a tough-minded, effective means of predictable behavior change.

Although, like every other new guru, the Behavior Therapists believe that it is *they* who will finally improve man's situation, their ministry derives not from a fascination with those struggles that have seemed most human, but from the observation of the behavior of laboratory animals. The principles that guide the learning of the animals are the same as those that apply to people, the differences being merely a matter of complexity. The behavior of every organism is an ultimately predictable response to a stimulus. Men and beasts are subject to the same processes of learning, and "most behavior is learned through a process called *conditioning*, by which links are established between certain stimuli and responses."[8]

The Behavior Therapists' work with patients is an attempt to bring about desired behavior by the programming of the sequence of rewards and punishments that establish such linkages between stimulus and response. Troubled people who seek help are viewed as having problems in social learning, as are troublesome people who the community insists need to be "helped." Both the painful anxieties of the help-seekers and the anxiety-producing "antisocial" behavior of those who have help thrust upon them are seen as symptoms to be removed.

Speculation about the meaning of their lives or about the underlying causes of their symptoms is set aside as fruitless fancy. One need only assume that neurotic symptoms are learned and that the proper programming of a new schedule of learning experiences will bring about any new combination of desired behaviors to take their place. There is nothing more to it, because "the so-called symptom *is* the neurosis."[9]

Behavior Therapists have researched the matter thoroughly and have "proved" that other forms of psychotherapy rarely work. (This may be another case of examining the anatomical structure of the bumblebee in the light of the principles of aerodynamics and so proving that it is physically impossible for the poor deluded creature ever to be able to fly.) When other forms of therapy are at all effective, it is because they unwittingly and unsystematically apply the principles of Behavior Therapy.

It is my impression that Behavior Therapy works best in changing those habit patterns that insight and existential types of psychotherapy are most helpless to change: autism, delinquency, compulsive patterns of nail-biting, bedwetting, phobias. It is difficult for me to imagine just what a Behavior Therapist would do for a patient of mine whose presenting problem is stated as: "I feel as though I don't really know who I am," or "My life just doesn't seem to have much meaning," or "I can't seem to love anyone deeply."

In accomplishing some of the considerable easing of human suffering to which they have seemed relevant, Behavior Therapists apply laboratory discoveries to the patient's practical problems. In contrast, the Psychoanalysts make discoveries while treating patients, which they then generalize into universal truths that are applied to mankind at large. The ways in which the Behavior Therapists apply these principles of learning fall into three major treatment methods: Reciprocal Inhibition, Aversion Therapy, and Operant Conditioning.

Reciprocal Inhibition is a method of Behavior Therapy retraining often used to treat phobias and other unreasonable anxieties. It is rooted in the classical conditioning work of Ivan Pavlov, a Russian physiologist, who experimented on dogs some fifty years ago. This form of learning is typified by the situation in which Pavlov rang a bell just before presenting food to hungry dogs. After repeating this sequence a number of times, he could merely ring the bell without presenting the food and still get the dogs to salivate (a kind of drooling ordinarily reserved for anticipation of eating). There are a number of alternative explanations for this irrelevant drooling. For us, it might be enough to settle for the notion that this classical conditioning teaches creatures to associate certain automatic or inborn responses to novel or artificial stimuli that have been presented along with their usual or natural evokers. For Pavlov's dogs, it was a matter of teaching an old response new stimuli.

Behavior Therapists contend that phobias are learned in a similar manner, that is, by having something inherently frightening associated with some innocuous stimulus, which in turn later evokes the fear by itself. So it is with the "laboratory neuroses" induced in rats that are shocked each time they are placed in a small cage. Eventually, just approaching such a cage evokes panicky behavior in these animals. However, it was discovered that if they were hungry enough and repeatedly fed nearer and nearer to such a small cage, they gradually become undisturbed by being in this formerly terrifying setting.

This finding led the originator of Reciprocal Inhibition to the contention "If a response antagonistic to anxiety can be made to occur in the presence of anxiety-evoking stimuli so that it is accompanied by a complete or partial suppression of the anxiety responses, the bond between these stimuli and the anxiety responses will be weakened."[10] Or, more simply, it is not possible to be relaxed and anxious at the same time. If we can help the patient to experience the things that frighten him at times when he can remain relaxed, eventually he will no longer be upset by those things or situations that originally caused him needless distress.

The fact that this treatment model originates with animal experiments would lead us to expect that the Behavior Therapist's role is simply that of change agent or controller of behavior, that a computer would do as well (if not better). The rhetoric of the Behavior Therapist supports this by playing down any importance of the personal relationship between therapist and patient. And yet the treatment of patients by Reciprocal Inhibition begins with hypnotic relaxation techniques, which require a good deal of trust and submission on the part of the patient.

Next, a hierarchy of anxieties is constructed by establishing a graduated list of frightening stimuli. For someone who has a phobia for cats this might range from looking at a picture of a little kitten who is playing in the distance, all the way up to holding a live, full-grown cat on his lap. The retraining consists of the Behavioral Therapist's getting the patient deeply relaxed and then having him imagine the weakest item on the list. This is repeated until it no longer makes him anxious. Then they go on to the next item, until session by session, the patient learns not to be afraid. This densitization can help make life once more bearable for people oppressed by irrational fears. Its proponents believe that even the most complex of maladaptive life styles are ultimately reducible to intricate systems of phobias, which can be differentiated and resolved in the same way.

Despite the hope that Reciprocal Inhibition would be able to change all sorts of behaviors, its use is usually restricted to the treatment of irrational fears. Repeated undesirable acts, "compulsive" symptoms such as sexual deviations, overeating, excessive gambling, and the like, are treated instead by means of *Aversion Therapy*. In such cases undesirable behavior has become a source of pleasure and satisfaction to the patient, and it is the therapist's job to link the stimulus for such acts to a new and unpleasant response, such as one aroused by the administration of painful electric shocks or nauseating drugs. An advocate of this method describes his treatment of an obese young woman in this way:

The electrodes having been attached to her left forearm, Miss H . . . was told to raise her right hand as soon as she had formed a clear imaginary picture of some desirable foodstuff. An almost unbearable current . . . was then instantly delivered and continued until she lowered her right hand as a signal that the shock could no longer be borne, as she usually did after a second or two.[11]

His objective, unapologetic, unsentimental description offers a sense of how, in the interests of technological improvement of man's lot, scientific detachment can shade over into a dehumanized handling of people as objects. Progress achieved under the guruship of Behavior Therapists could result in a society of smiling robots.

The third technique used by Behavior Therapists is *Operant Conditioning*, a system for selectively rewarding desired behavior, which stems from Harvard psychologist B. F. Skinner's work with pigeons. If a pigeon or a person performs some particular piece of behavior (pecking at a lever or being friendly to other people), then the experimenter or the therapist rewards that act (with a food pellet or a token that can be exchanged for ward recreation privileges).

The rewarded behavior becomes more and more likely to occur, while unrewarded behavior tends to drop out. Gradually, the ways in which people act can be shaped into the desired patterns. Operant conditioning has been especially helpful with recalcitrant, uncooperative patient populations such as delinquents and autistic children.

Like other forms of Behavior Therapy, the use of Operant Conditioning is subject to a chillingly detached objectivity. As a proof of the efficacy of this technique, one researcher was able to completely "extinguish" what had been nonstop delusional talk of a hospitalized paranoid woman by rewarding her only when she spoke sanely. The reward he used was to turn off an unpleasantly loud buzzer to which she was subjected when she talked crazy. To show how well this worked, he then reversed the process by rewarding the crazy talk instead: "He brought back her paranoid talk by punishing her whenever she spoke of normal topics."[12]

The work of the Behavior Therapists has brought a new willingness to try to evaluate the effects of psychotherapy more objectively. And too, these new gurus have helped many people who were previously considered to be hopelessly trapped in their unhappiness, troubled people whom Psychoanalysts too often seemed bent on explaining away as "resisting" cure (an easier answer than facing the inadequacies of their own approach).

There is great potential for corruption in the very scientific detachment that underlies the helpfulness of Behavior Therapy. Standing as he does somehow outside of and above ordinary human concerns, this new guru comes too easily to a sense either of knowing what is best for others or, paradoxically, of being the expert technician whose skills are at the service of any power. Pavlov's work has become the attempted basis for some Soviet and Red Chinese programs both of mental health and of political behavior control. Skinner, in turn, has contributed to the helpful treatment of heretofore hopeless patient populations. But he has also become the darling of those who would direct and control the behavior of workers who are to produce more, of consumers who are to buy more, and of social deviants who are to conform. Skinner is the hero of utopian hippie types who would set up an idyllic commune within which each could do his own thing. Paradoxically, he is' also the dupe of the Establishment from which they have dropped out.

HUMANISTIC PSYCHOLOGY

The Third Force, Humanistic Psychology, arose in part as a spirited outcry against the Psychoanalyst's smug reduction of man to nothing but an often sick compromise between chaotic instincts and repressive social forces, and against the Behavior Therapist's detached dehumanizing of man to the status of a technical problem to be solved, no different than a dog to be retrained.

This Third Force is sometimes called the "Human Potential Movement," but it is really too new, too diverse, too proudly unsystematic to provide an integrated, cohesive body of ideas or techniques. Fed by streams as diverse as Zen, progressive education, modern dance, and group dynamics research, the Third Force is more an attitude than a position, more an amalgam than a group. Its gurus and their supporters are in some ways a colorful ragtag band of yea-sayers with that great tolerance for differences among themselves that customarily marks spiritual pilgrimages at the outset of the journey. The "movement" consists of a loosely knit bunch of turned-on pilgrims, excited about being a part of a social alliance which espouses:

A centering of attention on the experiencing person. . . . An emphasis on such distinctively human qualities as choice, creativity, valuation, and self-realization. . . . An allegiance to meaningfulness in the selection of problems for study. . . . [and] An ultimate concern with and valuing of the dignity and worth of man and an interest in the development of the potential inherent in every person.[13]

As with other such young and hopeful seekers after a new and better world, members of the movement include a few beautiful, dedicated, creative leaders, many promising but as yet underdone aspirants, a substantial number of ordinary joiners (those who provide the bulk of financial support and do the public relations and the dog work), and a growing minority of the sort of kooks who seek instant intimacy and easy salvation, or worse yet, arise to provide these insubstantial wares to others in exchange for easy money and an ego trip.

The entire assemblage consists of people weary of the pessimism of the psychoanalytic emphasis on neuroses, universal complexes, and achievements that are "nothing but" compromise resolutions of underlying unconscious conflicts; and of people untrusting of the Behavior Therapy promise of a brighter tomorrow through the scientific manipulation of their heads, a promise of programmed happiness. But they are not only refugees who wish to escape from the oppression of earlier, now corrupted gurus. They are voyagers in search of joy. In search of ecstasy, they are hopeful, turned-on *people who would say yes to life.*

Three of the most charismatic gurus of the movement have been Abraham Maslow, Carl Rogers, and Fritz Perls; the Visionary, the Saint, and the Super-Star of Humanistic Psychology.

Abraham Maslow was one of the earliest of those psychologists who saw that it had been a mistake to study only "sick" people, problem situations, and unhappiness. Distortion must follow from looking only to evil as a model for man's future or as a source of understanding his nature. Maslow had the vision to see that recent gurus had been too much concerned with sorrow and not enough with joy, with sickness and not with health, with healing and not with growth, with adjustment and not with transcendence, too much with destructiveness and not enough with creativity.

He chose to study the creative, pro-life face of man, partly to redress the imbalance brought about by the earlier emphasis on the pathological. He also reacted against the movement to subsume the study of man under the model of the physical sciences. Instead, he was most concerned with the person as a singular, unique being whose humanness must not be lost in the service of some scientifically predictable, objective conception that washes out the colors of life. In our study of a man in his world, "the generic, the abstract, the rubricized, the categorized and the classified [must not obscure] the fresh, the raw, the concrete, the idiographic."[14]

Maslow brought together some of his vision of psychological health, of creativity, of being, in his concept of "self-actualization." People in trouble are motivated by deficits, by a need to make up for things they lack (such as protection, belonging, or affection). The more mature person, one whose basic needs have been gratified, no longer struggles to cope in the same way. Rather, the self-actualized man gives the picture of ease, spontaneity, and self-expression (in the place of neurotic tension, rigidity, and desperate seeking).

He is free to be "devoted to some task, call, vocation [or] beloved work outside of himself."[15] Though strongly ethical, identified with mankind, and capable of profound relationships with others, he is not concerned with what others may think of him. His quality of detachment, need for privacy, and self-acceptance may make him appear at times to be unfriendly, hostile, or simply selfish. He himself is past concerning his head with the distinctions between selfishness and unselfishness, between "I want to" and "I must," between work and play.

I first read Maslow's conception of self-actualization about 1950, when he passed around typewritten copies of an unpublished manuscript to some of us who were graduate students at Brooklyn College, where he taught. The experience was like having blinders removed from my eyes, allowing me to see in a way that filled me with hope. His exciting vision began to move me from my brooding immersion in the psychoanalytic world of neuroses and complexes.

And yet, in the midst of all of this, I found it distracting that some of the characteristics of the self-actualized man were so gratuitously idiosyncratic. For one, I remember that Maslow proposed that such a man would enjoy spending some time each day at a job such as shelling peas, so that his mind would be free to wander in creative fantasy. At first, this puzzled me. Then, all at once, I understood the seemingly irrelevant idiosyncrasies in this lovely, imaginative presentation of the model of the fully-human man. These characteristics were conclusions drawn from Maslow's study of a number of creative people. Yet this paradigm, perhaps like that of any psychological theorist, was in part autobiographical, or at least shaped by its author's own personal style and ideals. In his immersion in producing this idealized self-portrait, Maslow had simply forgotten to remove the moustache. What he had produced was a model which would inspire a generation of gurus, but he had left in some details that were no more than bits of his own personal eccentricities. Even in this foible, Maslow inadvertently teaches us something about what it is to be human.

Self-actualization is not an image of an elite, psychological aristocracy. Rather, each of us has had some peak experiences, some moments when we were open to the wonder of our own being and of the world. Think of your "happiest moments, ecstatic moments, moments of rapture, perhaps from being in love, or from listening to music or suddenly "being hit" by a book or a painting, or from some great creative moment."[16] Peak experiences such as these are "transient moments of self-actualization."[17] Ecstasy is available to everyone. And each of us can take charge of our lives in a way which will increase our chances for happiness. How many times, when faced with some decision about expressing our feelings or taking up some challenge, do we back off and kid ourselves that this is not the time or the place, that perhaps it would be better to wait? If we would become self-actualized, we must give ourselves to resolving such conflicts by "making the growth choice rather than the fear choice."[18] Maslow made this choice in spending his life in the study and affirmation of his dream of a world of greater happiness and more creativity, a world more human.

Carl Rogers, like Maslow, has brought hope in the form of a more optimistic, more trusting, more loving image of man. But Rogers is less a theoretician than a practitioner, a guru who inspires more with his ways than with his words. His major contribution to Humanistic Psychology is Client-centered Psychotherapy. His focus is on the client, the troubled person seeking help, and yet he has helped me most by throwing light on the feelings of the therapist, on the personhood of the guru.

Early in his work, Rogers grew dissatisfied with having the counselor's role defined as distant and superior, as the expert authority who handed down interpretations. He saw the client and the therapist as equals, and so felt that the therapist's attitude should be respectful, open, and permissive. The therapist's orientation must be phenomenological in that concern must be for the world as the client experiences it, rather than for "reality" (compared with what?) or as a screen for the "hidden" unconscious dynamics. In fact, Rogers felt that any diagnostic assumptions about the client would be presumptuous and detrimental. Instead the non-directive therapist treats the patient with "unconditional positive regard" and respects the client's feelings. He can show the client he is understood, and help him to understand his own feelings more clearly by reflecting back in a non-judgmental way, what the client has said. In such an atmosphere, Rogers believes the client will solve his own problems.

Rogers' own words give a feeling for the man and for what he teaches about what it means to be a guru:

> If I can create a relationship characterized on my part:
> by a genuineness and transparency, in which I am my real feelings;
> by a warm acceptance of and prizing of the other person as a separate individual;
> by a sensitive ability to see his world and himself as he sees them;
> Then the other individual in the relationship:
> will experience and understand aspects of himself which previously he has repressed;
> will find himself becoming better integrated, more able to function effectively;
> will become more similar to the person he would like to be;
> will become more self-directing and self-confident;
> will become more a person, more unique and more self-expressive;
> will be more understanding, more acceptant of others;
> will be able to cope with the problems of life more adequately and more comfortably.[19]

Rogers' profound humanness, his incredible gentleness, his heart-rending concern make it hard for me to listen to some of the tape recordings of his work with clients without feeling tears rise up behind my eyes. And yet I have felt even better about what Rogers is doing when, in later years, he began to come across as someone who helped others by being tough as well as tender.

If Maslow was the Visionary of Humanistic Psychology, and Rogers is its Saint, then Fritz Perls was its Super-Star. Perls was the founder of Gestalt Therapy, a complex theoretical non-system that departs radically from its psychoanalytic roots, differentiating itself by way of the German conception of Gestalt psychology. The latter point of view stresses the fact that we perceive in organized ways, meaningfully relating parts to the whole, and with a dynamic interplay between the figure on which we focus and the ground that serves as its context. Perls wrote a number of books attempting to define the brilliance of his position, but for most of us who have learned from him, his brilliance came across not in his expositions but in his performances.

In later years, Perls most often performed in a group, in which he would invite one member at a time to come and sit in the chair known as the "hot seat," to try to work out some personal problem. In such a group, you could learn what he meant in saying, "Nothing exists except in the here an now,"[20] in telling us we need only become aware of *how* we prevent ourselves from being free, and never mind *why* it came about. In such a group, Perls would turn one defensive, unhappy person after another away from intellectual "mind-fucking" words and help them to spill into the power of the moment. Neurotic problems are seen as unfinished business (incomplete *Gestalten*) that can only be solved in the present. All of the needed elements are present, but we keep ourselves from feeling and integrating them by means of empty chatter and unaccepted fantasies, and by having our bodies express these feelings through posture and movements that we then can ignore.

Perls had enormously powerful personal presence, independence of spirit, willingness to risk going wherever his intuitive feelings took him, and a profound capacity to be intimately in touch with anyone who was open to working with him. He not only taught but vividly demonstrated his conviction that no one was put on earth to live up to anyone else's expectations. If he and another could come together, he would join in with delight; if not, he could shrug it off and forget about it. He was responsible only to and for himself.

Both his impact as a charismatic guru and the ways in which his own behavior served as a model for others were enormously helpful. But perhaps his greatest genius lay in his creative flair for spinning off ways to disarm people, to bypass their empty words and their social devices, to help them to stop paralyzing themselves. Some of his ways have since become standard techniques for a generation of Humanistic Therapists and Encounter Group Leaders.

Some of his contributions come through clearly in his unique technique of dream analysis. The person in the hot seat who has recounted a dream is asked to retell it, playing the part of each aspect of the dream in turn. For example, one man told of a frightening childhood dream: "The scene is a ridge of mountains out here, and a flat desert with white sand . . . [a] very dark sky, with the moon casting a very pale light over everything. And there's a train track crossing the desert in a perfectly straight line. And the train is coming along."[21] Perls gets him to play each of the parts—to be, feel, speak for the desert, the ridge of mountains, the train tracks, and the train. The dreamer can act out each part or engage in dialogue alternating between one part and another. Each part of the dream is really a part of the dreamer. As he reclaims each disowned aspect of himself, he comes to be more alive, to feel more deeply, to be freer.

Watching such a dream analysis is not only fascinating and instructive, but even more, it catches up the other group members in the turmoil, the struggle, and the freeing. It is not unusual to find yourself in tears, or exhausted, or joyful, after watching another being guided through such an experience. So brilliant was his intuition and so powerful were his techniques that sometimes it took Perls only minutes to reach the person on the hot seat. You might be some stuck, rigid, long-dead character, seeking help and yet fearing that it would come and change things. He would put you on the hot seat and then do his magic. If you were willing to work, it was almost as though he could reach over, take hold of the zipper on your façade, and pull it down so quickly that your tortured soul would fall out onto the floor between the two of you.

Despite the power and the brilliance, such techniques are only good for openers, and much more work must be done if feelings are to be worked through and life to be lived more fully. Unfortunately, in the epidemic of encounter groups[22] which have been inadvertently generated by the gurus of Humanistic Psychology, there is much of the quality of a religious revival movement, the fundamentalist tent meetings that pervaded the rural and small-town South earlier in this century. "Growth Centers" have sprung up everywhere. Some are staffed by competent leaders and provide exciting, nurturant opportunities for people to actualize their potential in a setting that gives priority to their well-being. Too many others are no more than a home phone number, a pile of inspirational brochures, and a stable of self-ordained encounter preachers who will hold a tent meeting wherever the money and the adoration is available. Their ambitions are fed not only by the growing popularity and demonstrable worth of the Human Potential Movement, but by the increasing number of devoted "regulars," of experience-hungry encounter-group freaks who live from one marathon to the next.

Some of Fritz Perls's compellingly disarming Gestalt techniques and many of the other nonverbal Esalen-type group exercises are surprisingly easy to learn to use. So effectively do they bypass ordinary intellectual, verbal, and social defenses that they can put group members in disconcertingly immediate touch with powerful, often unfamiliar feelings, even when the techniques are applied by leaders who lack a depth of understanding of human struggles. Such experiences will probably not do great damage to the participants. People seem much tougher to me than they claim to be, especially people who insist that they are fragile or inadequate.

The greater danger lies in the parallel to the revivalistic tent meeting. Some of these circuit riders are unseasoned, lightweight leaders whose only credentials are a few weeks spent at a growth center with a big-name guru and a flair for the short con. Armed with group techniques as powerful as hellfire-and-damnation preaching and shoutin'-and-stompin' Gospel, they can turn on encounter group members to an experience as powerful and as temporary as a group experience of religious conversion. The combination of dramatic witnessing by the conversion-addicts and the group pressure to be saved puts many people through powerful changes, changes that last until about Wednesday.

The saddest part of this exploitation is the disappointment and the lost opportunities. It makes it harder for genuine seekers to know where to turn and for responsible group leaders to maintain public trust. The Human Potential Movement has made help available to people who would not have sought it elsewhere. It has brought more human contact and tenderness to some lonely souls who were rigidly encased in plastic social roles. It has given some of the timid the strength to dare to express themselves in the world. It has given some people who had already gotten their thing together an opportunity for further growth. Unfortunately, it has also misled too many people into taking a moving group experience to be a substitute for the difficult and prolonged work of straightening out their tangled lives and maintaining the freedom of their long-imprisoned selves.

So quickly has this proliferation of cardboard gurus come about in Humanistic Psychology that it seems that corruption may have become speeded up in this age of instant communication through mass media, particularly when what is offered is instant intimacy and immediate solutions to age-old struggles. Still Humanistic Psychology, it seems to me, holds much promise, particularly for people who would have remained untouched by the more elitist psychoanalytic efforts, and it does so without subjecting them to the brainwashing dangers of Behavior Therapy. Many people in the Human Potential Movement are keenly aware of how vulnerable the movement is to charlatanism and are struggling to solve this problem. Most seem less aware of the danger inherent in Humanistic Psychology itself. Part of its strength lies in the optimism of Maslow's focus on creativity and transcendence, and in Rogers' promotion of growth through self-acceptance; but strengths and weaknesses are often only different faces of the same singularity.

The corruption of the efforts of the gurus of Humanistic Psychology is likely to come from a daimonic surrender to their wish to achieve joy. They already, I feel, begin to ignore the darker side of man. Or at the very least, when man's finitude, his loneliness, his ambiguity, and the inevitability of decay of his efforts are not ignored, they are seen as problems which can eventually be overcome. Before the gurus of Humanistic Psychology crumble and yield to the next wave of revolutionary charismatic leaders, they may yet "turn on" many people. But if they presume to overcome the ambiguity of the human situation, they may turn themselves off prematurely.

15 The Refusal to Mourn

"After the first death, there is no other . . ."

—DYLAN THOMAS

And so it seems that wherever men have sought the counsel and guidance of other men, a creative minority of helpers, healers, and guides has arisen to meet this need. Though their words and their dress have differed in the many times and places in which they have appeared, these *gurus* have come forward as spiritual guides, as those special sorts of teachers who help other men to make their passage from one stage of their lives to another.

The Paleolithic Shaman, the Hasidic Zaddik, the Christian Desert Father, and the oriental Zen Master seem, at first, very different from one another. Yet as we come to know them, we can see how alike they are. Each is *the most extraordinarily human* member of his community. Each teaches by distracting the people he would help, by turning them away from conventional wisdom, by disrupting their "rational" everyday ways of understanding. Each instructs by being a person to his followers rather than by depending on the force of his formal office.

As with all human endeavors, the special sort of spiritual leadership that particular gurus provide always turns out to be ephemeral. Man's efforts are as real and as momentary as the lovely castles that little children so love to build out of wet sand at low tide. Each is given all that the child can bring in the way of grave concentration, joyful creativity, and sincere hope for eternal endurance. Working devotedly in the wet, dark sand, these little builders angrily push away other children who would ruin what they are trying to make. They cry heartbreakingly when some unthinking grown-up spoils their work with a ruinous imprint of a heavily-planted bare foot. And yet, too soon, no matter what, the tide will inch up the beach to eat away with quiet inevitability what each child has created in his mad trust of the moment.

Gurus and their followers also build sand fortresses to stand against the eternal rhythms of the tides. Like the children, sometimes they secretly know that their spiritual castles will not stand against the tide, a tide which has retreated only to advance once more. Like the children, they may know that their creations are built in the area of unrest that is the human present, and that after the ebb comes the flood tide. And yet, who knows? Perhaps, they insist, this one time something permanent can be built.

It is through this insistence, this willing what cannot be willed, that children (whatever their ages) often bring on the very ruination that they hope, for once, to avoid. The children, having brought about a fairy castle where once there was only shapeless mud, could go on developing and living in fantasy in what they have built until they have to give way to the restless sea. Instead, at this point, they too often give their efforts over to building protective embankments, hopeless ramparts to stand against the sea. They rake the mud this way. They rake the mud that way. In the time they are brooding over it, they could be stringing pearls for the delight of heaven.

And worse yet, in the frantic building of walls against the coming of the sea, the castles are often ruined by those who hope to perpetuate their existence. In these pitiable efforts at carving something permanent out of the marginal world of ever-changing, never-changing Nature, the original intent is often lost sight of. How much wiser to let Nature flow through us than to try to separate ourselves out to stand against it.

Gurus have come—and gone—often to leave something behind, something worth keeping, something of their style, of their technique, of their sense of what is needed, or simply of what is most human. Each worked well for a while—in his own time, in his own place. Then the leadership of each became institutionalized, daimonically exaggerated, idolized. Their teachings became ossified, reified, diluted, popularized. The gurus themselves were corrupted by their own arrogance. Their followers became faddists, cultists, believers in a way aimed at making the meaning of life fully clear, once and for all, forever.

Part of what we can learn from these magic moments of the past is that ours too shall pass. If we try to hold on to that past, insisting that it must not be lost to us, then we shall fall more quickly and more ignobly than did the gurus of the past whom we would preserve. We may get what we can from our own present efforts to struggle with what human happiness is all about, but only if we see that we too can develop nothing lasting. We must give up what cannot last and what we cannot change, accepting our losses, if we are to have all that we might of present meanings and joys.

We must feel as sad and helpless as we need to, and then we must go on. Hasidism teaches us:

There are two kinds of sorrow. . . . When a man broods over the misfortunes that have come upon him, when he cowers in a corner and despairs of help—that is a bad kind of sorrow. . . . The other kind is the honest grief of a man whose house has burned down, who feels his need deep in his soul and begins to build anew.[1]

The struggles in our dealing with the problems of what we must give up and what we may retain from the gurus of the past may be likened to each man's struggles with his own personal history. Within the perspective of my own sort of psychotherapy, this acceptance of helplessness, this need to mourn, is just as much mine as it is theirs who seek my help.

The reason for this is that, to some extent, each of us still lives in the darkness of his own unfinished past. The refusal to mourn the disappointments and losses of childhood, to bury them once and for all, condemns us to live in their shadows. Genuine grief is the sobbing and wailing that express the acceptance of our helplessness to do anything about losses. If instead we whine and complain, insist that this cannot be, or demand to be compensated for our pain, then we are forever stuck with trying to redeem the past.

Psychotherapy is basically a difficult moral venture. It is the attempt by the therapist to help the patient to become and to live as a decent human being, no matter how hard a time he has had. He must learn to live well, in the present, beginning with things as they are, and open to the many ambiguities of this mixed bag of a world as it is. And all of this he must do in spite of the fact that he has been cheated, has had to stand by helplessly while he was ignored, betrayed, undone; while he watched his hopes shattered, his most precious possesssions lost, and his dreams unrealized. What is more, if he refuses to accept the misfortunes of the past as unalterable, then he does not get to keep the warm, loved feelings intact. These joys of yesterday and of now will be open to being somehow spoiled whenever he feels helpless about some new loss.

Perhaps there are only different kinds of unhappy childhoods, and remembrances of happy childhoods are merely illusions desperately held on to. Children are, after all, inevitably helpless and dependent, no matter what resources they may develop for coping with that towering world in which they live. Parents always turn out to be a disappointment, one way or another. Frustrations are many, and life is inherently unmanageable. "Momma may have, Poppa may have, but God bless' the child that's got his own, that's got his own."*

As children, we are all really helpless to change our worlds or to move on and take care of ourselves when we cannot. Unable to give up hope on such a life-and-death matter, the child is confronted with the desperate anxiety that results from trying to will that which cannot be willed. Each child finds ways of pretending to himself that he is not as powerless as he feels. He must maintain the illusion that somehow he can get his parents to love him as he wishes to be loved. Panic over his helplessness must be transformed into a stubborn struggle to get his own way , even if only in fantasy. The more he has been treated as though his feelings did not count, the greater his own resultant willfulness. It is in the service of maintaining the illusion that he can get his own way, that his neurotic behavior is endlessly and irrelevantly repeated and that self-restricting, risk-avoiding character styles develop.

In this way to varying degrees, people insist that the world has to be fair, that either they must get what they want or else someone must pay. Thus, for example, an obsessively worried young man points out that he can never be happy, never really free to enjoy his successes, because he was raised by so mean and selfish a father and so undependably vague a mother. His suffering is their indictment, and he won't let them off the hook.

A hysterical young woman insists that since she has had to put up with disappointments in the past, certainly by now some wonderful person must come along and take care of her.

Another tells us of what a very awful person she is. It is not that mother was selfish or unloving, but rather just that even as a little girl she was too bad, abnormal, or somehow unsatisfactory to warrant better treatment. And now if she can only improve enough, things with Mamma would have/could have/will be different.

Yet another fellow goes the opposite route, showing how little he needs others, how uncaring and above it all he is. If only he had good Le Bret, that friend of Cyrano's to whisper to him, "Be proud and bitter, but underneath your breath—whisper 'she loves me not—and that is death.' "[2]

There are, of course, many and varied ways in which adults may continue to play out these childhood struggles. What they have in common is limited commitment to the meaning of their lives as it stands. Rather, their common outcry is: "I've been cheated and I won't

*"God Bless' the Child," by Arthur Herzog, Jr., and Billie Holiday (1941). Copyright, Edward B. Marks Music Corporation; used by permission.

stand for it. I must have my way. If not, at the very least, others will not get their way with me again." The adult in whom the unmet, unmourned child dwells stubbornly insists that he has the power to make someone love him, or to make them feel sorry for not doing so. Appeasing, wheedling, bribing, or bullying are carried out in stubborn hope that if only he is submissive enough, sneaky enough, bad enough, upset enough, something enough—then he will get his own way.

Part of the therapist's task is to avoid getting entangled by the patient's attempts at emotional blackmail, intimidation, seductive adoration, dependent demands, and the like. Of course, the therapist is likely to be hooked into responding to these maneuvers in some ways, but then the recognition and disentangling get the patient to begin looking at what he is up to. The therapist tries to arouse the patient's curiosity about his own life. At the same time that the therapist is interrupting these self-defeating strategies by not going along with them, he is also insisting on being recognized as a person in his own right, with feelings that count. He must find ways to let the patient know that:

My pain hurts as your does. Each of us has the same amount to lose—all we have. My tears are as bitter, my scars as permanent. My loneliness is an aching in my chest, much like yours. Who are you to feel that your losses mean more than mine. What arrogance! . . . I feel angry at your ignoring my feelings. I live in the same imperfect world in which you struggle, a world in which, like you, I must make do with less than I would wish for myself. . . . And too, you seem to feel that you should be able to succeed without failure, to love without loss, to reach out without risk of disappointment, never to appear vulnerable or even foolish. . . . Why? While the rest of us must sometimes fall, be hurt, feel inadequate, but rise again and go on. Why do you feel that you alone should be spared all this? How did you become so special? In what way have you been chosen? . . . You say you've had a bad time of it, an unhappy childhood? Me too. You say that you didn't get all you needed and wanted, weren't always understood or cared for? Welcome to the club!

The therapist must help the patient to see that for each of them, this session is an hour of his life, no more to be recaptured by the one than by the other. They could become important to one another, but only to the extent that each disarms himself, takes the chance of being vulnerable to being hurt by the other, of risking new losses.

As the interaction focuses the patient's attention on past losses and on what he has to lose in the encounter with the therapist, he must be left no quarter. He can only keep what he really had. When he insists that his parents loved him "in their own way," he must be faced with the realization that this is an inference. When parental love is offered in a form that takes the child's feelings into account, it can be experienced directly by the child. It does not need to be inferred. And if the patient did not get what he wanted or needed or was entitled to simply because he was their kid, that's rough, but that's it.

All he can do now is try to face how really bad he feels and how stuck he is with it. Then he may turn to others in his life and try to be open enough so that they may get to know him. He can make his wishes known, and if they come through, fine. If not, if they know him but don't love him, then there's nothing to be done about it. Perhaps someone else will love him. But in any case, no one can take anyone else's place. It will never be made up to him. He will just have to do without, like it or not, and face his losses and his helplessness to change them. He must weep, and mourn, and grieve them through. He must unhook from the past to make room for the present. In burying the parents of childhood, he must make do with the rest of the world minus two. Not such a bad trade after all.

By no longer refusing to mourn the loss of the parents he wished for but never had, he can get to keep whatever was really there for him. He may come to know that not getting his own way does not always mean he is not loved. No longer living in the seemingly ordered world of childhood, in which good and suffering are supposed to be rewarded and evil and selfishness punished, he must nonetheless try to do his best to live decently. An unhappy childhood is not a justification for copping out. Life is a mixed bag, at best, for everyone. Each man must face disappointment, frustration, failure, loss and betrayal, illness, aging, and finally his own death. And yet he must face up to Camus' challenge: *"to be a just man in an unjust world."*[3] You find life arbitrary and yet take things as they are, bring to them what you can, and enjoy them as they stand. This is it, often unsatisfying, at times disappointing, always imperfect. But it's the only world we have. Can you be loving in it and bring to it the meaning of your own being and willingness? Can you live without illusions in a world where there is no appeal? Can you love in the absence of illusions?

In order to take up this challenge, deceptively simple insights too fundamental to be grasped once and for all must be learned, not just once, but renewed again and again. As Hemingway tells us,

"There are some things which cannot be learned quickly, and time, which is all we have, must be paid heavily for their acquiring."[4]

As though it were not enough to struggle with the arbitrary parameters of childhood, once free of them, each man must realize other elusive truths such as: Each of us is, in his own terms, vulnerable. Each is as weak and as strong as the other, as tough and as tender, as capable of good and of evil, and consequently, each is as fully responsible for his actions as the other. And too, it is very exciting and terribly hard to be a grown-up human being (perhaps almost as hard as it is to be a child).

As a grown-up, *ultimately each man is alone.* No one can do for him what he must do for himself.

> You got to walk that lonesome valley,
> You got to walk it by yourself;
> Nobody else can walk it for you,
> You got to walk it by yourself.[5]

No other's solution will do. Each man has to contend with the same fundamental condition of being *here*, and *now*, and *himself and no other*. Yet for each it is different, even while being the same. It differs mainly in that I am not you, though our plight is the same.

Each man's relation to every other man is ironically drawn in Samuel Beckett's novel, *Molloy*.[6] This two-part tale begins by telling of Molloy, the antihero—a dirty, unkempt, snot-dripper; a crippled, festering, rag-clad derelict wandering without purpose; a scatological consciousness and a social shamble. His journey in exile reduces him still further, till he is no longer simply misfit, degenerate, and outcast, but also put upon, beaten, and almost killed. Even his crutches are of little use when he ends up alone, still homeless and now exhausted, barely managing to crawl through the snowy forest night toward the light of the plains far in the distance, perhaps toward shelter, warmth, or maybe even home.

The second part of the novel tells of Moran, a man of consequence who has and is everything Molloy has not and is not. He has a home and a family, a place in the church and in the community. He is clean, well-tailored, barbered, and manicured, altogether well turned out. He also has an assignment: "Get Molloy." Without knowing just why, or on whose orders, he sets out to see about fulfilling this obligation. He is never sure whether or not he has found him, though it may, in fact, have been Molloy whom at one point he beat and almost killed. But in his pursuit of Molloy, Moran ends up losing his way, is separated from his family and his position, is attacked and injured so that he must use his umbrella as a crutch. And finally, unshaven, uncombed, unwashed, and hungry, his clothes in tatters, he ends up alone, homeless, and exhausted, barely managing to crawl through the freezing night rain toward a house far in the distance, which he hopes will provide shelter, warmth, or maybe even home.

Thus, we had best come to know one another, for there is little else for us in this world. We must each learn what it is we have to give to the other, and what it is we may hope to receive. It is so very hard sometimes to be a human being: a grown-up, limited, at times helpless, take-care-of-yourself-'cause-no-one-else-will individual person. What can we hope to be for one another in this frightening, exciting world in which we are both free and trapped? What I hope to give to my patients—and what I also hope to get from my patients—is the courage and comfort of knowing someone else who faces his life as it is, risks the knowing, feels what I feel, struggles as I struggle, mourns his losses—and survives.

We must live, I believe, in the face of knowing that man is ultimately not perfectible. Evil can be redistributed but never eradicated. Each solution creates new problems, and the temptation to cop out is ever present. Perhaps all that we can hope for is to be committed to the struggle to do our best as much as we are able. And the relationship between patient and therapist, between man and man, is a community of sinners. Loving and joyful though we may sometimes be, "the wish to kill is never killed, but with some gift of courage one may look into its face when it appears, and with a stroke of love—as to an idiot in the house—forgive it; again and again . . . forever."[7]

By mourning our losses and burying our dead, in therapy and in the rest of life, we open ourselves to the only real contact we can have with others—touching now, standing in the rubble of the past. For we are all Jews. We all wander in exile. We suffer, trying to believe that there is a reason. We try to go our way and to do what is right. But at times each of us forgets. We want some certainty, some clarity. We want the face of the enemy at last to be clear and for the good guys to win once and for all. At that point, when any man forgets that he is a Jew, denies that he is in exile—at that point he runs the risk of becoming a Nazi. In his quest for home, for permanence, for clarity and dependable meaning, he may define himself by becoming the one who defines others, defines them as Jews by persecuting them, or more insidiously, by separating himself from them and denying common humanity.

Our only hope is as a community of exiles. Wanderers are Jews, wherever they are from, whatever their religion. They are exiles from the illusions of childhood, the illusion of the all-good family and of the certain place in a world that makes sense. It matters not whether a man is self-exiled in response to disappointment and in search of a more meaningful place, a promised land; or whether another man has had the original comforting illusion violently wrenched away. What matters is that the loss of innocence is permanent. There is no returning. There is only the community of wanderers, the touching of hands by passing exiles.

And so too, this is the way it must be as we stand our losses in the face of the decay of promises and hope offered by the gifted gurus of the past. We must learn from them, even from their failure and their corruption. But we must not expect that we ourselves will be able to transcend the human limits of momentary spiritual grace, grace from which we each must surely fall. Though, if we accept the inevitability of our fall, we may rise again. To be reborn, one first must die.

What, then, can present and future gurus learn from the gurus of yesterday? Today's secular psychotherapist is not the saint-mystic the Zaddik was. He cannot give himself over to the visionary trance of the Shaman. He does not aspire to the devoted austerity and solitude of the Desert Father. And yet, each of the gurus of the past has something to teach him about his own attempts to help other people.

Let me speak of Hasidism, at its best, in these terms. For the hasid, his Zaddik's entire way of being was illuminating, compelling, and capable of raising him up the rungs of the spiritual ladder toward reunion with God. For the unhappy person who comes to a psychotherapist for help, there is, instead, the secular teacher whose healing powers are redemptive in the sense that they help return the patient to himself and to the world. It is not the therapist's holiness and exemplary life but rather his way of being with himself and with the other during the hour that mediates the patient's recovery and growth.

Perhaps what the Zaddik teaches me as a therapist is that I will surely fail if I try to help a troubled person by starting out from a position of detachment. Instead, I must begin by simply being willing to be with him, to get to know him as another person, and to let him come to know me. I must trust my feelings over my knowledge and live out the truth rather than try to perceive it. I must be willing to tremble without retreating from the possibility of being personally vulnerable to him simply as another human being, of risking his becoming truly important in my life.

The patient and the psychotherapist must come to know each other in ways that are singular to this meeting of these two particular human beings. Only then will the one who is seeking guidance find himself able to work successfully at solving the problems in his life, problems that up till then have kept him from being at one with himself and open to being with others. Not only will this be a useful experience for the patient, but the therapist, too, will find himself renewed and expanded.

Certainly, as a therapist, I may also advise, teach, interpret, support, offer a model, selectively reinforce, and undo with counter-strategies. But if all of this occurs outside the context of genuine personal engagement, in the absence of loving, then all that I do is to teach new games, perhaps more effective games, but games nonetheless.

I am deeply grateful for my encounter with the Zaddik, the Baal Shem Tov of Hasidism, and with all of the other gurus out of history and legend, gurus of the past and of the present. They have illuminated my own life. The most valuable of the gifts that I have received from them is the courage to be my own sort of guru, to work toward doing the kind of psychotherapy in which I am most free to become who I am.

When Rabbi Noah, Rabbi Mordecai's son, took his father's place as Zaddik, his followers soon saw he behaved differently from his father. They were troubled and came to ask him about this. "But I do just as my father did," he replied. "He did not imitate, and I do not imitate."

Hard Travelin'

"I've been doin' some hard travelin',
I thought you know'd.
I've been doin' some hard ramblin',
Away down the road.
Hard travelin', hard ramblin',
Hard drinkin', hard gamblin',
I've been doin' some hard travelin', Lord."*

—WOODY GUTHRIE

(This is an account of a hellish journey I made during the writing of Guru. *Men and women who had sought my help as a psychotherapist made part of that journey with me. I have included this epilogue to offer testimony to my own experience of the relationship between the contemporary guru and those to whom he would offer guidance.—S.K.)*

Over the last several years of working as a psychotherapist, I have come more and more often to reveal myself to particular patients at particular times. Most often it has to do with some fantasy or something out of my own life, which is evoked by my experience of being with the patient. This has made therapy a richer, more renewing experience for me and has often seemed meaningful for the patient.

Most recently, I have been into something so serious, comprehensive, and preoccupying, that I have chosen to discuss it with all of my patients, in groups and individually. The problem was physical but had many overwhelming feelings related to it.

About three years ago, I suffered a sudden and profound hearing loss in my left ear. It was diagnosed correctly as irreversible nerve deafness but was mistakenly attributed to an exotic, highly selective virus. Hearing aids were of no use, and after a brief period of panic

*Hard Travelin'. Words and music by Woody Guthrie. TRO – © Copyright 1959 and 1963 by Ludlow Music, Inc., New York, New York. Used by permission.

(lest I lose the hearing in my other ear), I adjusted with counterphobic insistence that other people recognize my limitation; sorry they had to contend with it, but after all I give a good deal, and there was no reason why they couldn't help out by speaking up.

Then during the summer of 1969, I developed vertigo—a highly discomforting loss of balance, experienced as the world spinning about while my legs gave out beneath—brought about by sudden head movements, and eventuating in a general sense of unsteadiness on my feet. This was worrisome and had the quality of having a taken-for-granted parameter of reality suddenly falling away. Still I discussed this only very selectively with patients and only when it somehow came to the fore.

It did, however, lead me to a series of diagnostic tests at one of the local university hospitals and raised the specter of a possible tumor. That centered it for me. Head surgery seemed likely. I became preoccupied with the feeling that I might well die; and even if I were to survive, the idea that people were going to stick knives into the inside of my head brought feelings of being violated, of ending up brain damaged, of recovering to find that I would no longer be myself. As the clinical evidence accumulated, I could see that even if all went fairly well, I might have to disrupt my practice for one or two months, maybe longer. But more than that, I was very upset. And I had weeks of waiting to get through.

I did not decide in advance that I would discuss my troubles with everyone. I simply brought them up in one group when I could think of nothing else—I did not want my depression experienced as a reaction to the group (which it was not). I told the group members simply and directly what was going on and how I felt. By this time my reactions included worry, grief, fear, anger, and a deep sense of helplessness. I denied my feelings of helplessness with dreams and fantasies of my own crazy wish to perform the operation on myself while instructing others in the technique. Discussing this bit of craziness and some of the consequent destructive rejecting of help offered by people who loved me was something I offered as a gift to a patient in one group. She had long been very frightened and ashamed of her own secret craziness. In response to my sharing, she revealed more of herself and then brought tears to my eyes by taking my hand and kissing it.

Almost all of my patients were very interested in learning all they could about my plight. There were, of course, some initial denials: "It's so hard to imagine that something really bad could happen to anyone as strong as you," or "You're too good, your head is too much together, for something so terrible to just come on you." Just a very few patients were much more willfully evil about it: "It's too upsetting to let myself think about it. I don't believe it's really going to happen." One frightened woman went so far as insisting: "I just know that there is nothing to worry about, that everything is going to turn out all right." She had difficulty for a long while in understanding why my rejoinder was, "Fuck you, too."

Most of the responses were far more loving: "I'm so touched that you would share such big trouble with us," or "I am so worried about what will happen to you," or "You must be so upset," or "I'm scared for you and for me," or "I wish I could protect you from this." There was, as well, much in the way of tears and touching (theirs and mine) and even the giving of good luck charms. Some patients felt overwhelmed at what I must face and had trouble not feeling guilty about their concerns for themselves. Few could freely express resentment directly toward me for being less than they had hoped, though some could rail against the fates and acknowledge that this was not a good time for them for this to have happened.

Even before my first hospitalization, there were so many hours of complicated dialogue interspersed with respectful silences that I am finding it difficult to document it in an orderly fashion. Some sessions do hold together well, such as one group session spent on the recounting by each of us of our hospital experiences and what they meant to us, with everyone learning something new about what the experience could be for another. The best testimony that I have as to what went on during those pre-hospital discussions is my recollection of their effects on me. I felt warmly grateful and deeply loved. I found new ways to accept my importance in the lives of some other people. I realized how much more some patients meant to me than others did. I felt both the support that would help me to face my own fear and unhappiness, as well as the insistent courage of many patients whose willingness to face things as they were helped to keep me honest when I would rather have fled from some of what I feared.

It was certainly not that I was entirely without all this outside of my practice. My wife was magnificently helpful, as I will later describe. And there were some loving friends who gave much at the cost of having to make some of my anguish their own, to all of whom I am deeply grateful. With my patients, however, there was a new intimacy, an unfamiliar sense of community, and my first positive experience of extended family. While I was away, there were some gifts and many letters. I rarely received them without feeling touched to the point of tears. They were rarely routine expressions of conventional feelings, but rather almost always were rooted in the real history of our relationships.

My first hospitalization was by far the easier of the two. This was to be an attempt to remove part of the tumor by acoustical surgery so as to reduce the risks which would accrue if total removal were to be attempted in a single neurosurgical procedure. The hospital was in a city hundreds of miles from home, as there were few surgical teams in the country that were experienced in this particular set of procedures. Only my wife was with me during the surgery, but she is one of the crucial centers of my life. I wanted no one else there.

The setting was just right—an old-timey, nursing staff-dominated hospital cluttered with arbitrary rules, allegedly for the patients' benefit but clearly to make things easier on the staff. Especially during the preoperative days of further diagnostic testing, this afforded me just the sort of challenge I needed to assert the impact of my personal identity as a way of escaping from how scared and helpless I felt. The staff could not believe me as I successfully changed rooms, bypassed arbitrary rules, and shaped some of what went on to my feelings as a particular human being rather than as an hypothetical patient. The operation itself went very well, and I was sent home only four days later to recover enough to be operated on again.

Though I was greatly fatigued and had some head pain, being at home again was a lovely experience. I had not originally expected to be home for the holidays, and so we had attempted an early Christmas celebration which the whole family tried to pretend was working out. Actually we all felt lousy, cheated, done in. Now we had a real family Christmas; oh, not so noisy or exuberant as usual, but warm and comforting, grateful and protected and safe. Friends visited, and there were for a while only good feelings. But gradually, as time for the next operation early in January drew nearer, our apprehensions began to grow. My dreams were no longer compensatorily strong and free. Now they had a trapped quality which bespoke both how caught I really was and how paranoid I would eventually become. I avoided seeing, or talking on the phone with, any of my patients because I felt stuck in the middle with little more that I could do but dump my upset on them and all over myself. But their letters were welcome and more touching than I could have imagined.

The second surgical expedition was far different from the first. The second hospital was larger and more modern, the nursing staff more sophisticated and more urbane. If anything, this left me less arbitrary administrative structure with which to hassle in order to distract myself from my fears. And too, this was to be neurosurgery—"very serious." Again my wife was on the scene; this time her presence would be crucial. During the first couple of days of presurgical observation and preparation, I found another patient to whom I could superficially relate as a therapist, thus putting off experiencing myself as a patient for a while. But that was soon to come.

On the morning of the third day I entered surgery, mostly fearing that I might end up with some of the predicted sequelae of facial paralysis and disfigurement and/or weakness and numbness, that is, crippling, of my left side. I emerged from the operating room twelve hours later, not only alive but without any apparent sequelae. True, they had to leave a small piece of the tumor on the brainstem, because each time the surgeon tried to remove it, my pulse stopped. But this had been anticipated, and it might well slough off from lack of blood supply, simply not grow, or grow again after some years and require still another operation (the doctors seemed to have no idea what caused tumors or stopped or stemmed their growth). All in all, it seemed that my particular future was merely more clearly uncertain than that of most other people.

But it was not to be so easy as all that. Brain swelling and failing respiration led to a "medical crisis" in which I was rushed back to the recovery room where I would be treated with drugs and other conservative means, or from which I could be rushed for further surgery (perhaps including the removal of part of my cerebellum). My wife Marjorie was trying to make decisions too hard for anyone to make for another, scared to death, yet having to remain composed enough not to be labeled "hysterical" and shunted off out of the way. She was sufficiently effective to be allowed to remain and participate in my nursing care.

I spent much of the next two days in the recovery room. This is an intensive care unit with bright, unwavering overhead lights. Slipping back and forth between sleep and pain, I found myself surrounded by strange equipment, much of which was painfully attached to me. Strange, large, gowned figures appeared and disappeared, shouting in my face as though I were a very young retardate, "Your operation is over. What's your name? Do you know where you are?" And no one would explain to me just what was going on. The combination of whatever problems I brought to the situation, the disorienting effects of the recovery room, adverse reaction to the morphine compounds I had been given, and a typical response to massive neurosurgery (a bit like getting hit on the back of the head with a telephone pole), all resulted in my being wildly psychotic for about two days. Whatever the immediate causes of the episode, it was clearly shaped by unresolved pieces of craziness which I brought to it.

To begin with, I was confused, terrified, could not understand, and did not know if it would ever end. A bad trip. I was sure they were trying to hurt me. They had put some device into my nose; it hurt and so I pulled it out. It was bloody, and then I was sure they were trying to kill me. Because I interfered with their efforts, they tied down my hands (later I learned that this was done with gauze, but then I thought I had been chained). I felt helpless, enraged, humiliated. I tried to punch one of the nurses in the face. In retrospect, I realize that I must have been a pain in the ass to them, that they continued to try to help, and that I must have correctly read the resentment behind their attempts to reassure me that they really wanted to help me. But I was too smart for them. I knew. I became more and more cunning in tricking them into removing some of the torturous breathing devices they had put on me.

Some of my perceptions became more elaborate but not clear. The hospital seemed somehow anti-Semitic and my persecution a part of that. Some of the equipment seemed Jewish and all right, but some of it seemed Christian and worried me. Also, though I wanted to sleep, I visualized this as some sort of a "tableau" being set up so that if I slept, the videotape footage of my sleeping would be used as comic relief in whatever kind of TV show this was that they were putting on. At last I recognized my wife at my bedside. She took my hand, and I knew I could trust her. I told her to get an investigating committee from the American Civil Liberties Union to check on their tying my hands without due process. She realized that I was crazy and just kept repeating to me in her way, "Look, darling, you're mixed up. They are all doing what they're doing to help you. I know it hurts and you can't understand it right now, but you know I wouldn't let them do anything bad to you. Just try to cooperate and rest."

And by God, it worked. I feel so accepted by her and trust her love so much that I would feel deeply at peace, settle down, and stop fighting the staff. But each time I fell asleep, I woke up crazy again. Each time she was able to reassure me. Luckily, when I was upset before the operation—that is, tearful and worried—I told her that I did not want to spill over openly in this setting lest I end up being fucked over by some young psychiatric resident (who might have thought me crazy even if he had spoken to me at my most sane). Remembering this, though with many doubts, she did not tell the staff of all the craziness I gradually shared with her. And so I was eventually released without being committed, bombed out on drugs, or given any further "care."

Once home, I felt for a while as though I were on fugitive status. At the same time I felt relieved to have survived and fortunate to be left with such trivial losses (a bit of facial numbness, some subtle discoordination of my left hand, and still some vertigo, all of which gave promise of eventually passing). A bit at a time I began to feel like myself, as intact physically and spiritually as I had before the operation.

Some weeks later I began seeing my patients again. Because they had been able to check on my progress only through contacts with my co-therapists, they did not know of all I had been through. Communications between the hospital in Boston and my friends in Washington had been fragmentary, at times confused, and usually erred in favor of positive reporting. Almost everyone was clearly glad to see me, seemed at first relieved, and was eventually shocked to hear the recounting of what had in fact gone on.

Indeed, there was for everyone, including myself, less a feeling of joy than a deep sense of relief. It had been a hard way to go. Clearly, I had survived. Not only did I yet live, but what was more, I seemed intact—in short, "myself." Despite the ordeal and the uninvited suffering to which those patients who felt close to me had been subjected, most felt "glad to have been included." Some few, of course, regretted the whole episode, had good feelings that it was over, and wanted to dismiss the whole thing, being singularly uncurious as to what I had been through. These were the more covertly angry people who would rather not love than be bothered by the suffering of another.

Many people felt that this had been a very useful experience for them in that it helped to prepare them for their own catastrophes as well as making them aware that they had some options and responsibilities even in the face of situations which they largely could not control. One patient expressed very well what a number of others had been through. She said, "I so often felt tempted to put you out of my mind. After all, I couldn't do anything about the situation. Sometimes I just wanted to make up my mind that everything was sure to be all right and to forget it. Instead, for the first time in my life, I really let myself live with all my feelings of helplessness and uncertainty. It was very hard, but it makes me feel so good about myself. I was able to be myself without making excuses, and I feel so good about me now. Also, I was doing what I had learned in therapy. It was a way of saying how much I care about you—and about me."

Some people both wanted and did not want to hear the upsetting parts. But most agreed that my sharing made me seem more human to them. In fact, by revealing so much of my own still unresolved feelings and problems, I made some patients feel freer and more hopeful about themselves. If I were still so imperfect, perhaps they did not have so far to go. And too, now that I was well, more of the past anger came out directly. The patients' anger erupted at me for letting them down and abandoning them by being sick, and I could now shake my fist at the heavens for dealing me such an unwarranted and unexpected blow.

Over the years, before all of this, I had come to feel that I was at last (and always had been) all right, just as I was. Increasingly much of my life experience included feelings that I was warm, decent enough, strong, and more lovable than I had ever felt during the long years of growing up. Faced with possible crippling and disfigurement, I had gotten hung up on the feeling that I did not ever want to be in a position in which people would have to do for me because they felt sorry for me. Only after a long while did I come to understand that I feared if I were not in a position to give or to achieve, perhaps no one would want to bother about me.

After the worst of it was over at the hospital, I had a moving experience with one of the special duty nurses. She was an unlikely person for me to feel close to, but she tried hard to do the kind of job she felt she should do and to make my life more bearable. In the morning she would bathe me in her strong yet gentle way. It felt good after so much pain and so much impersonal handling. Suddenly I realized that as a child I had never been handled so well and with so much care. We talked, and she was glad I appreciated what she was doing, but it was very hard for her to understand why I should be crying. Now, with all that I have been given in tenderness, anguish, and loyalty, by my wife, my kids, my friends, and even by my patients, I believe I feel more loved than ever before in my life. I hope I can hold on to the feeling.

It is clear to me that my motives in writing of these experiences go far beyond my wish to share with other therapists what is for me a new approach with my patients. The very act of writing all this down, of telling my story, has certainly been helpful to me in getting myself together again.

Furthermore, I hope this account has the quality not only of personal confession, but of a celebration of well-loved others as well. I also realize that I may well be naïvely exposing my own unresolved problems to the eyes of others. Let it be! Every one of us has some hard travelin' to do. Now, I've been some bad places and I've seen some bad things, and I thank the Lord that not all of that hard travelin' has to be done alone.

S.B.K.
January–February 1970

Chapter Notes

PART I

Chapter One

1. Arnold J. Toynbee, *A Study of History*, 2 vols. (New York: Dell Publishing Co., A Laurel Edition, 1:288.
2. Sigmund Freud, "The Psychotherapy of Hysteria," *Studies in Hysteria* (London: Hogarth Press, Standard Edition, 1893), p. 305.
3. Leonard Cohen, "Suzanne Takes You Down," *Selected Poems, 1956–1968* (New York: Viking Press, A Viking Compass Book, 1968), p. 209.
4. Erich Fromm, *The Forgotten Language, An Introduction to the Understanding of Dreams, Fairy Tales and Myths* (New York: Rinehart & Co., 1951).
5. Ibid., p. 33.
6. *Oxford English Dictionary*, 1961, s.v. "charisma."
7. I Cor. 13:1.
8. Ibid., 13:2.
9. Ibid., 14:2.
10. Max Weber, *From Max Weber, Essays in Sociology*, trans. and ed. H. H. Gerth and C. Wright Mills (New York: Oxford University Press, A Galaxy Book, 1958), pp. 295ff.
11. Matthew Lipman and Salvatore Pizzurro, "Charismatic Participation as a Sociopathic Process," *Psychiatry* 1 (February 1965): 249.
12. Weber, *Essays in Sociology*, p. 237.
13. Mat. 5:17.
14. Ibid., 5:21.
15. Ibid., 5:20, 22, 26, 28, 32, 34, 38, 44.
16. Weber, *Essays in Sociology*, p. 249.
17. Lipman and Pizzurro, "Charismatic Participation," p. 18.
18. Dylan Thomas, *The Collected Poems* (New York: New Directions, 1953), p. 173.

Chapter Two

1. Max Weber, *From Max Weber, Essays in Sociology*, trans. and ed. H. H. Gerth and C. Wright Mills (New York: Oxford University Press, A Galaxy Book, 1958), p. 426.
2. Jay Haley, "The Art of Psychoanalysis," *The Power Tactics of Jesus Christ, and Other Essays* (New York: Grossman Publishers, 1969), p. 4.

3. Paul Goodman, "Can Technology be Humane?", *The New York Review of Books,* 13 (20 November 1969): 27–34. (my italics)
4. Leonard Krasner, "The Therapist as a Social Reinforcement Machine," *Research in Psychotherapy,* Volume II, ed. Hans H. Strupp and Lester Luborsky (Washington, D.C.: American Psychological Association, 1962), p. 61. (my italics)
5. Vin Rosenthal, "Each Therapist Creates Psychotherapy in his Own Image," *Voices,* 5 (Fall/Winter 1969–1970): 18.

Chapter Three

1. Joseph R. Royce, "Metaphoric Knowledge and Humanistic Psychology," *Challenges in Humanistic Psychology,* ed. James F. T. Bugental (New York: Mc-Graw-Hill, 1967), p. 27.
2. James Dickey, "Metaphor as Pure Adventure" (Lecture delivered at the Library of Congress, Washington, D.C., 1968), p. 2.
3. Susanne K. Langer, *Philosophy in a New Key* (New York: New American Library, A Mentor Book, 1952), p. 120.
4. Owen Thomas, *Metaphor and Related Subjects* (New York: Random House, 1969), p. 4.
5. Langer, *Philosophy in a New Key,* p. 119ff.
6. Dickey, "Metaphor as Pure Adventure," p. 9.
7. Langer, *Philosophy in a New Key,* p. 111.
8. Ibid, p. 164.
9. Ibid., p. 228.
10. Dylan Thomas, *The Collected Poems* (New York: New Directions, 1953), p. 15.
11. Ibid., pp. 194ff.
12. Ibid., p. 124.
13. Henry M. Pachter, *Paracelsus: Magic into Science* (New York: Henry Schuman, 1951), p. 63.
14. Dickey, "Metaphor as Pure Adventure," pp. 12ff.
15. M. H. Abrams, *The Mirror and the Lamp: Romantic Theory and the Critical Tradition* (New York: W. W. Norton & Co., 1958), p. 57.
16. Vincent F. O'Connell, "Until the World Become a Human Event," *Voices* 3 (Summer 1967): 75–80.

PART II

Chapter Four

1. Victor W. Turner, "An Ndembu Doctor in Practice," *Magic, Faith, and Healing,* ed. Ari Kiev (London: Free Press of Glencoe, 1964).
2. Joseph Campbell, *The Masks of God: Primitive Mythology* (New York: Viking Press, 1968), p. 240.

3. Arnold van Gennep, *The Rites of Passage* (Chicago: University of Chicago Press, Phoenix Books, 1964), p. 108.

4. Campbell, *Masks of God*, p. 238.

5. Andreas Lommel, *Shamanism: The Beginnings of Art*, trans. Michael Bullock (New York: McGraw-Hill, 1967), p. 39.

6. Baldwin Spencer and F. J. Gillen, *The Native Tribes of Central Australia* (London: MacMillan & Co., 1899); quoted in Campbell, *The Masks of God: Primitive Mythology* p. 255.

7. Lommel, *Shamanism*, p. 69.

8. S. F. Nadel, "A study of Shamanism in the Nuba Mountains," *Reader in Comparative Religion, An Anthropological Approach*, ed. William A. Lessa and Evan Z. Vogt (Evanston, Illinois: Row, Peterson & Co., 1958), p. 439.

9. Ibid., p. 437.

10. Ibid., p. 151.

11. Mircea Eliade, *Shamanism: Archaic Techniques of Ecstasy* (New York: Random House, Pantheon Books, 1964), p. 24.

Chapter Five

1. Moses Maimonides, "For the Sake of Truth," *A Jewish Reader*, ed. Nahum N. Glatzer (New York: Schocken Books, 1966), pp. 47–51.

2. Maurice S. Friedman, *Martin Buber: The Life of Dialogue* (New York: Harper & Row, 1960), p. 17.

3. Gershom G. Scholem, *Major Trends in Jewish Mysticism* (New York: Schocken Books, 1965), p. 131.

4. Ibid., p. 120.

5. Ibid., p. 132.

6. David Bakan, *Sigmund Freud and the Jewish Mystical Tradition* (New York: Schocken Books, 1965), pp. 76ff.

7. Scholem, *Jewish Mysticism*, p. 135.

8. Martin Buber, *Tales of the Hasidim: The Later Masters* (New York: Schocken Books, 1966), p. 87. (Buber's writings are the sources for all Hasidic stories referred to in this book.)

9. Scholem, *Jewish Mysticism*, p. 329.

10. Martin Buber, *The Origin and the Meaning of Hasidism* (New York: Harper & Row, 1966), p. 48.

11. Martin Buber, *Hasidism and Modern Man* (New York: Harper & Row, 1966), pp. 157ff.

12. Ibid., p. 165.

13. Buber, *The Origin and the Meaning of Hasidism*, p. 181.

Chapter Six

1. William A. Clebsch and Charles R. Jaekle, *Pastoral Care in Historical Perspective: An Essay with Exhibits* (New York: Harper & Row, A Harper Torchbook, 1967), p. 4. (italics omitted)

2. Mark 1:40–42.

3. Ibid., 5:7–14.

4. John 8:3–5 and 7:9–11.

5. Mat. 16 and 19.

6. John 20 and 23.

7. Clebsch and Jaekle, *Pastoral Care in Historical Perspective*, p. 59.

8. O. Hobart Mowrer, *The New Group Therapy* (Princeton, New Jersey: D. Van Nostrand Co., An Insight Book, 1964), pp. 17ff.

9. Ibid., pp. 97, 165ff.

10. F. Scott Fitzgerald, "Absolution," *The Stories of F. Scott Fitzgerald*, ed. Malcolm Cowley (New York: Charles Scribner's Sons, 1951), pp. 159–172.

11. Thomas Merton, "The Spiritual Father in the Desert Tradition," *The R. M. Bucke Memorial Society Newsletter-Review* 3 (Spring 1968): 19.

12. *The Desert Fathers*, trans. Helen Waddell (Ann Arbor, Michigan: University of Michigan Press, 1957), p. 66.

13. Merton, "The Spiritual Father in the Desert Tradition," p. 17.

14. *The Desert Fathers*, p. 13.

15. Ibid., p. 15.

16. Ibid., p. 13.

17. Merton, "The Spiritual Father in the Desert Tradition," p. 15.

18. *The Desert Fathers*, p. 16.

19. Ibid., p. 90.

20. Merton, "The Spiritual Father in the Desert Tradition," p. 11.

21. *The Desert Fathers*, p. 62.

22. Merton, "The Spiritual Father in the Desert Tradition," p. 66.

23. *The Desert Fathers*, p. 13.

24. Merton, "The Spiritual Father in the Desert Tradition," p. 124.

25. Ibid., p. 73.

26. Ibid., p. 107.

27. Ibid., pp. 106ff.

28. Ibid., p. 77.

29. Ibid., p. 103.

30. *The Desert Fathers*, p. 19.

31. *Meister Eckhart: A Modern Translation*, ed. and trans. Raymond B. Blakney (New York: Harper & Row, 1941), p. xxiii.

32. *Meister Eckhart*; quoted in F. C. Happold, *Mysticism: A Study and an Anthology* (Baltimore: Penguin Books, 1967), p. 72.

33. *Meister Eckhart*, p. 21.

34. Ibid., p. 253.

35. Ibid., p. 143.

36. Ibid., p. 245.

37. Ibid., p. 251.

Chapter Seven

1. *The Teachings of the Compassionate Buddha*, ed. E. A. Burtt (New York: New American Library, Mentor Religious Classics, 1955), pp. 44ff.

2. D. T. Suzuki, *Zen Buddhism: Selected Writings*, ed. William Barrett (Garden City, New York: Doubleday & Co., 1956), p. 30.

3. Chuang Tzu, *Basic Writings*, trans. Burton Watson (New York: Columbia University Press, 1964), p. 3.

4. Thomas Merton, *The Way of Chuang Tzu* (New York: New Directions, 1965), p. 89.

5. Ibid., p. 87.

6. Chuang Tzu, *Basic Writings*, p. 4.

7. Ibid., pp. 29ff.

8. Ibid., p. 45.

9. Ibid., pp. 48ff.

10. Merton, *Way of Chuang Tzu*, p. 156.

11. Arthur Waley, *Three Ways of Thought in Ancient China* (Garden City, New York: Doubleday & Co., 1956), p. 48.

12. Ibid., p. 67.

13. Merton, *Way of Chuang Tzu*, p. 15.

14. Confucius, *The Wisdom of Confucius*, trans. and ed. Lin Yutang (New York: Modern Library, 1943), pp. 9ff.

15. Ibid., p. 164.

16. Lao Tzu, *The Way of Life (Tao Te Ching)*, trans. Raymond B. Blakney (New York: New American Library, 1955), p. 19.

17. Christmas Humphreys, *Buddhism* (Harmondsworth, Middlesex, England: Penguin Books, A Pelican Book, 1951), p. 181.

18. Suzuki, *Zen Buddhism: Selected Writings*, pp. 111ff.

19. *Zen Flesh, Zen Bones: A Collection of Zen and Pre-Zen Writings*, comp. Paul Reps (Garden City, New York: Doubleday & Co., 1961), pp. 64ff.

20. Ibid., p. 96.

21. Ibid., pp. 59ff.

Chapter Eight

1. Henri Frankfort et. al., *Before Philosophy, The Intellectual Adventure of Ancient Man* (Harmondsworth, Middlesex, England: Penguin Books, A Pelican Book, 1951), pp. 250ff.

2. Ibid., p. 237.

3. Plato, *The Dialogues of Plato*, trans. B. Jowett, 2 vols. (New York: Random House, 1937), 1:112.

4. Rollo May, "The Delphic Oracle as Therapist," *The Reach of Mind: Essays in Memory of Kurt Goldstein*, ed. Marianne L. Simmel (New York: Springer Publishing Co., 1968), p. 211.

5. Ibid., p. 212.

6. John A. Crow, *Greece: The Magic Spring* (New York: Harper & Row, 1970), p. 86.

7. Ibid., p. 186.

8. Ibid., p. 137.

9. Plato, *Dialogues*, pp. 150ff.

10. John R. McNeill, *A History of the Cure of Souls* (New York: Harper & Row, A Harper Torchbook, 1965), p. 32.

11. Lucius Annaeus Seneca, *Moral Essays*, trans. John W. Basore, 3 vols. (London: William Heinemann, 1928–36), 1:41.

12. Ibid., 1:41ff.

13. Ibid., 2:417.

14. Ibid., 2:419ff.

15. Ibid., 2:357.

16. Ibid., 2:391.

Chapter Nine

1. Niccolo Machiavelli, *The Prince and the Discourses* (New York: Modern Library, 1950), p. 91.

2. Ibid., p. 94.

3. Ibid., p. xiv.

4. Joseph Anthony Mazzeo, *Renaissance and Revolution: The Remaking of European Thought* (New York: Random House, 1965), p. 72.

5. Machiavelli, *Discourses*, pp. 77ff.

6. Ibid., pp. 64ff.

7. Mazzeo, *Renaissance and Revolution*, pp. 143ff.

8. Baldesar Castiglione, *The Book of the Courtier*, trans. George Bull (Baltimore, Maryland: Penguin Books, 1967), pp. 46ff.

9. Ibid., pp. 51ff.

10. Michel de Montaigne, *Selected Essays*, trans. Charles Cotton and W. Hazlitt and ed. Blanchard Bates (New York: Modern Library, 1949), p. 548. (In the original text, the second line appears first.)

11. Ibid., p. 563.

12. Ibid., p. 267.

13. Ibid., p. 285.

14. Ibid., p. 602.

15. *Paracelsus: Selected Writings*, ed. Jolande Jacobi and trans. Norbert Guterman (New York: Pantheon Books, 1951), p. 29.

16. Henry M. Pachter, *Paracelsus: Magic into Science* (New York: Henry Schuman, 1951), p. 11.

17. Ibid., p. 7.

18. *Paracelsus: Selected Writings*, p. 79.

19. Ibid., p. 57.

20. Ibid., p. 138.

21. Pachter, *Paracelsus: Magic into Science*, p. 63.

Chapter Ten

1. A. A. Milne, *Winnie-the-Pooh* (New York E. P. Dutton & Co., 1926, 1954), p. 38.

2. Ibid., pp. 40ff.
3. Ibid., p. 28.
4. L. Frank Baum, *The Wizard of Oz* (Chicago: Reilly & Lee Co., 1956), pp. 120ff.

Chapter Eleven

1. Aldous Huxley, *Brave New World* (New York: Bantam Books, 1967), p. 30.
2. Ibid., p. 36.
3. George Orwell, *Nineteen Eighty-four* (New York: New American Library, 1964), p. 202.
4. Ibid., p. 225.
5. Ibid., p. 211.
6. Ibid., p. 220.
7. Robert Sheckley, "The Minimum Man," *Store of Infinity* (New York: Bantam Books, 1970), p. 82.
8. Ibid., p. 93.
9. Ray Bradbury, "Swing Low, Sweet Chariot," *Psychology Today* 2 (April 1969): 43.
10. Ibid., p. 44.

Chapter Twelve

1. R. E. L. Masters and Jean Houston, *The Varieties of Psychedelic Experience* (New York: Dell Publishing Co., A Delta Book, 1967), p. 131.
2. Ibid., p. 143.
3. Ibid., pp. 146ff.
4. Ibid., p. 132.
5. Lewis Yablonsky, *Synanon: The Tunnel Back* (Baltimore, Maryland: Penguin Books, A Pelican Book, 1965), p. vii.
6. Ibid., p. 150.
7. Carl R. Rogers, "The Process of the Basic Encounter Group," *Challenges of Humanistic Psychology*, ed. J. F. Bugental (New York: McGraw-Hill, 1967), pp. 261–276.
8. Hobart F. Thomas, "Encounter—The Game of No Game," *Encounter: The Theory and Practice of Encounter Groups*, ed. Arthur Burton (San Francisco: Jossey-Bass, 1969), p. 77.
9. Ibid., p. 76.
10. Ibid., p. 78.
11. William Barrett, *Irrational Man: A Study in Existential Philosophy* (Garde City, New York: Doubleday & Co., 1962), p. 13.

PART III

Chapter Thirteen

1. Dylan Thomas, *The Collected Poems* (New York: New Directions, 1953), p. 1.
2. Ibid., p. 21.
3. Ibid., p. 113.
4. Ibid., p. 10.
5. Ibid., p. 6.
6. Ibid., p. 15.
7. Ibid., p. 9.
8. Ibid., p. 14.
9. Albert Camus, *The Rebel*, trans. Anthony Bower (Harmondsworth, Middlesex, England: Penguin Books, A Pelican Book, 1962), p. 269.
10. Thomas, *Collected Poems*, p. 77.
11. Ibid.
12. Ibid., p. 128.
13. Ibid., p. 130.
14. Ibid., p. 1.
15. Ibid., p. 13.
16. Max Weber, *From Max Weber, Essays in Sociology*, trans, and ed. H. H. Gerth and C. Wright Mills (New York: Oxford University Press, A Galaxy Book, 1958), pp. 54ff.
17. Arnold J. Toynbee, *A Study of History*, 2 vols. (New York: Dell Publishing Co., A Laurel Edition, 1965), 1:359.
18. Weber, *Essays in Sociology*, p. 54. (my italics)
19. Toynbee, *Study of History*, 1:606.
20. Weber, *Essays in Sociology*, p. 55.
21. Albert Camus, cited in *I. F. Stone's BiWeekly*, 6 April 1970.
22. Rollo May, *Love and Will* (New York: W. W. Norton & Co., 1969), p. 123.
23. Toynbee, *Study of History*, 1:356ff.
24. James Agee, *The Morning Watch* (New York: Ballantine Books, 1966), p. 107.
25. Ibid., p. 109.

Chapter Fourteen

1. Sigmund Freud, *A General Introduction to Psychoanalysis*, trans. Joan Riviere (Garden City, New York: Garden City Publishing Co., 1943), p. 17.
2. Herbert Marcuse, *One-Dimensional Man* (Boston: Beacon Press, 1964).
3. Phillip Reiff, *Freud: The Mind of the Moralist* (Garden City, New York Doubleday & Co., An Anchor Book, 1961), p. 361.

4. Sigmund Freud, *The Basic Writings of Sigmund Freud*, trans. and ed. A. A. Brill (New York: Modern Library, 1938), p. 207.

5. Reiff, *Freud*, p. 188.

6. Ibid., p. 371.

7. Perry London, *The Modes and Morals of Psychotherapy* (New York: Holt, Rinehart & Winston, 1964), p. 43.

8. Hans J. Eysenck, "New Ways in Psychotherapy," *Readings in Clinical Psychology*, cont. ed. Barbara A. Henker (Del Mar, California: CRM Books, 1970), p. 66.

9. Ibid., p. 72.

10. Joseph Wolpe, *Psychotherapy by Reciprocal Inhibition* (Stanford, California: Stanford University Press, 1958), p. 71.

11. Ibid., p. 182.

12. Eysenck, "New Ways in Psychotherapy," p. 73.

13. Charlotte Buhler and James F. T. Bugental, untitled pamphlet (San Francisco: Association for Humanistic Psychology, 1970).

14. Abraham Maslow, *Toward a Psychology of Being* (Princeton, New Jersey: D. Van Nostrand Co., An Insight Book, 1968), p. 137.

15. Abraham Maslow, "A Theory of Meta-motivation: The Biological Rooting of the Value-Life," *Readings in Humanistic Psychology*, ed. Anthony V. Sutich and Miles A. Vich (New York: Free Press, 1969), p. 155.

16. Maslow, *Toward a Psychology of Being*, p. 71.

17. Abraham Maslow, "Self-Actualization and Beyond," *Challenges in Humanistic Psychology*, ed. James F. T. Bugental (New York: McGraw-Hill, 1967), p. 283.

18. Ibid., p. 282.

19. Carl R. Rogers, *On Becoming a Person* (Boston: Houghton Mifflin Co., 1961), pp. 37ff.

20. Frederick Perls, *Gestalt Therapy Verbatim*, comp. and ed. John O. Stevens (Lafayette, California: Real People Press, 1969), p. 41.

21. Ibid., p. 90.

22. See my earlier discussion in Chapter 9 of Part II.

Chapter Fifteen

1. Martin Buber, *Tales of the Hasidim: The Early Masters* (New York: Schocken Books, 1966), p. 231.

2. Edmond Rostand, *Cyrano de Bergerac*, act 2.

3. Albert Camus, "Letters to a German Friend," *Resistance, Rebellion and Death* (New York: Modern Library, 1960), pp. 3–25.

4. Ernest Hemingway, *Death in the Afternoon* (New York: Charles Schribner's Sons, 1932), p. 192.

5. *Lonesome Valley*, A Spiritual in Public Domain.

6. Samuel Beckett, *Molloy* (New York: Grove Press, 1955).

7. Arthur Miller, *After the Fall*, act 2.

Suggested Reading

WORLD HISTORY

McNeill, John T. *A History of the Cure of Souls*, New York: Harper & Row, A Harper Torchbook, 1965 (Orig. ed.: New York: Harper, 1951).

Toynbee, Arnold J. *A Study of History*. 2 vols. New York: Dell Publishing Co., A Laurel Edition, 1965 (Orig. ed.: New York: Oxford University Press, 1947).

Weber, Max. *From Max Weber, Essays in Sociology*. Translated, edited, with introduction by H. H. Gerth and C. Wright Mills. New York: Oxforc University Press, A Galaxy Book, 1958 (Orig. ed.: New York: Oxford University Press, 1946).

METAPHOR

Dickey, James. "Metaphor as Pure Adventure." Lecture delivered at the Library of Congress, 1968, Washington, D.C.

Fromm, Erich. *The Forgotten Language, An Introduction to the Understanding of Dreams, Fairy Tales and Myths.* New York: Rinehart & Co., 1951.

Langer, Susanne K. *Philosophy in a New Key*. New York: New American Library, A Mentor Book, 1952, 1956 (3rd ed.: Cambridge: Harvard University Press, 1957).

Thomas, Dylan. *The Collected Poems of Dylan Thomas*. New York: New Directions, 1953.

Thomas, Owen. *Metaphor and Related Subjects*. New York: Random House, 1969.

PRIMITIVE RELIGION

Campbell, Joseph. *The Masks of God: Primitive Mythology*. New York: Viking Press, 1959, 1968.

Eliade, Mircea. *Shamanism: Archaic Techniques of Ecstasy*. Translated by Willard R. Trask. 2nd ed. New York: Random House, Pantheon Books, 1964.

Lommel, Andreas. *Shamanism: The Beginnings of Art*. Translated by Michael Bullock. New York: McGraw-Hill, 1967.

Nadel, S. F. "A Study of Shamanism in the Nuba Mountains." In *Reader in Comparative Religion, An Anthropological Approach.* Edited by William A. Lessa and Evan Z. Vogt. Evanston, Illinois: Row, Peterson & Co., 1958.
Turner, Victor W. "An Ndembu Doctor in Practice." In *Magic, Faith, and Healing.* Edited by Ari Kiev. London: Free Press of Glencoe, 1964.
van Gennep, Arnold. *The Rites of Passage.* Translated by Monika B. Vizedom and Gabrielle L. Caffee. Chicago: University of Chicago Press, Pheonix Books, 1964 (Orig. ed.: Chicago: University of Chicago Press, 1960).

JUDAISM

Bakan, David. *Sigmund Freud and the Jewish Mystical Tradition.* New York: Schocken Books, 1965 (Orig. ed.: Princeton, N. J.: Van Nostrand, 1958).
Buber, Martin. *Hasidism and Modern Man.* New York: Harper & Row, 1966 (Orig. ed.: New York: Horizon Press, 1958).
———. *The Origin and the Meaning of Hasidism.* New York: Harper & Row, 1966 (Orig. ed.: New York: Horizon Press, 1960).
———. *Tales of the Hasidim: The Early Masters.* New York: Schocken Books, 1947.
———. *Tales of the Hasidim: The Later Masters.* New York: Schocken Books, 1948.
———. *Ten Rungs: Hasidic Sayings.* New York: Schocken Books, 1947.
Maimonides, Moses. "For the Sake of Truth." From Commentary on the Mishnah. In *A Jewish Reader.* Edited by Nahum N. Glatzer. 2nd ed. New York: Schocken Books, 1966 (Orig. ed.: *In Time and Eternity,* New York: Schocken Books, 1946).
Scholem, Gershom G. *Major Trends in Jewish Mysticism.* New York: Schocken Books, 1965 (3rd rev. ed.: London: Thames and Hudson, 1955).

CHRISTIANITY

Clebsch, William A. and Jaekle, Charles R. *Pastoral Care in Historical Perspective: An Essay with Exhibits.* New York: Harper & Row, A Harper Torchbook, 1967 (Orig. ed.: Englewood Cliffs, N. J.: Prentice-Hall, 1964).
The Desert Fathers. Translated with introduction by Helen Waddell. Ann Arbor, Michigan: University of Michigan Press, Ann Arbor Books, 1957 (Orig. ed.: New York: Barnes and Noble, 1936).
The Holy Bible, King James Version. Philadelphia: John Winston Company.
Meister Eckhart: A Modern Translation. Translated and edited by Raymond B. Blakney. New York: Harper & Bros., 1941.
Merton, Thomas, "The Spiritual Father in the Desert Tradition," *The R. M. Bucke Memorial Society Newsletter-Review,* Spring, 1968, pp. 7-21.

THE ORIENT

Chuang Tzu. *Basic Writings*. Translated with introduction by Burton Watson. New York: Columbia University Press, 1964.

Confucius. *The Analects of Confucius*. Translated and annotated by Arthur Waley. New York: Random House, A Vintage Book, 1938 (Orig. ed.: New York: Hillary House).

———. The Wisdom of Confucius. Translated and edited with notes by Lin Yutang. New York: Random House, Modern Library, 1943.

Lao Tzu. *The Way of Life (Tao Te Ching)*. Translated by Raymond B. Blakney. New York: New American Library, A Mentor Religious Classic, 1955.

Merton, Thomas. *The Way of Chuang Tzu*. New York: New Directions, 1965.

The Teachings of the Compassionate Buddha. Edited by E. A. Burtt. New York: New American Library, A Mentor Religious Classic, 1955.

Waley, Arthur. *Three Ways of Thought in Ancient China*. Garden City, New York: Doubleday & Co., An Anchor Book, 1956 (Orig. ed.: New York: Macmillan, 1940).

Watts, Alan. *Beat Zen, Square Zen and Zen*. San Francisco: City Lights Books, 1959.

Zen Flesh, Zen Bones: A Collection of Zen and Pre-Zen Writings. Compiled by Paul Reps. Garden City, New York: Doubleday & Co., An Anchor Book, 1961 (Orig. ed.: Rutland, Vt.: C. E. Tuttle Co., 1958).

ANCIENT GREECE AND ROME

Frankfort, Henri; Frankfort, H. A.; Wilson, John A.; and Jacobsen, Thorkild. *Before Philosophy: The Intellectual Adventure of Ancient Man*. Harmondsworth, Middlesex, England: Penguin Books, A Pelican Book, 1951 (Orig. ed.: *The Intellectual Adventure of Ancient Man*, Chicago: University of Chicago Press, 1946).

May, Rollo. "The Delphic Oracle as Therapist." In *The Reach of Mind: Essays in Memory of Kurt Goldstein*. Edited by Marianne L. Simmel. New York: Springer Publishing Co., 1968.

Otto, Walter F. *Dionysus: Myth and Cult*. Translated with introduction by Robert B. Palmer. Bloomington, Indiana: Indiana University Press, 1965.

Plato. *The Dialogues of Plato*. Translated by B. Jowett with introduction by Raphael Demos. New York: Random House, 1937.

Seneca, Lucius Annaeus. *Moral Essays*. Translated by John W. Basore. London: William Heinemann, 1928–36 (Cambridge: Harvard University Press, the Loeb Classical Library, 1928–32).

THE RENAISSANCE

Castiglione, Baldesar. *The Book of the Courtier*. Translated with introduction by George Bull. Baltimore, Maryland: Penguin Books, 1967.

Machiavelli, Niccolo. *The Prince and the Discourses.* Introduction by Max Lerner. New York: Random House, Modern Library, 1950 (*The Prince,* translated by Luigi Ricci, revised by E. R. P. Vincent; London: Oxford University Press, 1906).

Montaigne, Michel de. *Selected Essays.* Translated by Charles Cotton and W. Hazlitt and revised, edited, with introduction by Blanchard Bates. New York: Random House, Modern Library, 1949.

Pachter, Henry M. *Paracelsus: Magic into Science.* New York: Henry Schuman, 1951.

Paracelus: Selected Writings. Edited with introduction by Jolande Jacobi and translated by Norbert Guterman. 2nd ed. New York: Pantheon Books, 1951.

TALES FOR CHILDREN

Baum, L. Frank. *The Wizard of Oz.* Chicago: Reilly & Lee Co., 1956.

Milne, A. A. *Winnie-the-Pooh.* New York: E. P. Dutton & Co., 1926, 1954.

SCIENCE FICTION

Bradbury, Ray. "Swing Low, Sweet Chariot," *Psychology Today,* April 1969, pp. 43–45. (Orig. published in Playboy, 1967, as "The Lost City of Mars").

Huxley, Aldous. *Brave New World.* New York: Bantam Books, 1967 (Orig. ed.: New York: Harper & Bros., 1932).

Orwell, George. *Nineteen Eighty-four.* New York: New American Library, 1964 (Orig. ed.: New York: Harcourt, Brace & World, 1949).

Sheckley, Robert. "The Minimum Man." In *Store of Infinity.* New York: Bantam Books, 1970.

THE "NOW SCENE"

Masters, R. E. L. and Houston, Jean. *The Varieties of Psychedelic Experience.* New York: Dell Publishing Co., A Delta Book, 1967 (Orig. ed.: New York: Holt, Rinehart & Winston, 1966).

Rogers, Carl R. "The Process of the Basic Encounter Group." In *Challenges of Humanistic Psychology.* Edited by James F. Bugental. New York: McGraw-Hill, 1967.

Thomas, Hobart F. "Encounter—The Game of No Game." In *Encounter: The Theory and Practice of Encounter Groups.* Edited by Arthur Burton. San Francisco: Jossey-Bass, 1969.

Yablonsky, Lewis. *Synanon: The Tunnel Back.* Baltimore Maryland: Penguin Books, A Pelican Book, 1965 (Orig. ed.: New York: Macmillan, 1965).

PSYCHOANALYSIS

Freud, Sigmund. *The Basic Writings of Sigmund Freud.* Translated and edited
with introduction by A. A. Brill. New York: Random House, Modern
Library, 1938.
———. *A General Introduction to Psychoanalysis.* Translated by Joan Riviere
with preface by Ernest Jones and G. Stanley Hall. New York: Boni &
Liveright, 1920.

BEHAVIOR THERAPY

Eysenck, Hans J. "New Ways in Psychotherapy." In *Readings in Clinical Psychology.* Edited by Barbara A. Henker. Del Mar, California: CRM Books,
1970.
Wolpe, Joseph. *Psychotherapy by Reciprocal Inhibition.* Stanford, California: Stanford University Press, 1958.

HUMANISTIC PSYCHOLOGY

Bugental, James F. T., ed. *Challenges in Humanistic Psychology.* New York: Mc-
Graw-Hill, 1967.
Maslow, Abraham. *Toward a Psychology of Being.* 2nd ed. Princeton, New Jersey:
D. Van Nostrand Co., An Insight Book, 1968.
Perls, Frederick. *Gestalt Therapy Verbatim.* Compiled and edited by John O.
Stevens. Lafayette, California: Real People Press, 1969.
Rogers, Carl R. *On Becoming a Person.* Boston: Houghton Mifflin Co., 1961.
Sutich, Anthony V. and Vich, Miles A., ed. *Readings in Humanistic Psychology.*
New York: The Free Press, 1969.